STAUBS AND DITCHWATER

A Friendly and Useful Introduction to Hillfolks' Hoodoo

H. Byron Ballard (signature)

H. BYRON BALLARD

D1452503

Smith Bridge Press

ASHEVILLE, NC

2nd ed. Edited by D. A. Sarac
Cover and book design by Diotima Mantineia
Inset cover photo by the author

Contact author at:
Asheville's Village Witch
www.myvillagewitch.com

ISBN #978-0-9767581-8-1

Smith Bridge Press
Asheville, NC
smithbridgepress@gmail.com

Special thanks to my readers and to the

writing group that calls itself

The Ecstatic Four.

Gratitude to my inspirations:

Nancy Dillingham, Vicki Lane, Celia Miles,

MariJo Moore, Linda Rago

This book is dedicated to my hoodoo guinea pigs
Bryan, Catherine, Diotima, Heatherly, Jennifer, Jo, Joe,
Machaela, Marcianne, Nina, Sabra, Star, Teresa, and
to the folks who found it interesting enough to want
a lecture, essay, or workshop—Denise Alvarado, Peg
Aloi, Hannah Johnston, Caroline Kenner, Tish Owen.

Firstly and lastly, this book is for all those wise and
wrinkled women who have always held the life of the
community in their rough hands. And for Jill.

Fresh, exciting, and brilliantly written, Byron Ballard's *Staubs and Ditchwater* is the perfect remedy to get your Mojo going again!
-Dorothy Morrison, author of *Utterly Wicked*

Like an Appalachian Brigit, Ballard tends an eternal fire. It's a flame that warms the hearth, but it's also a blaze that fuels a devotion to social justice. Her authority doesn't come from her degrees and her training (though she has them indeed) but from deep within her bones and within the earth of her home hills. If you want to experience an authentic traditional practice, turn these pages and find your reward.
-K. A. Laity, author of *Pelzmantel and Other Tales of Medieval Magic*

Byron Ballard, who is a brilliant teacher and an exciting, brilliant author.
-Judika Illes, author of *The Encyclopedia of 5000 Spells* and *Magic When You Need It*

At long last, an uncompromising primer in the folk traditions of the people of the Appalachian Mountains. *Staubs and Ditchwater: a Friendly and Useful Introduction to Hillfolks' Hoodoo* is written in an engaging, conversational style that will have you feeling as if you are walking with the author down by the crick picking herbs, digging up roots, and talking about things to come. Congratulations to H. Byron Ballard for successfully illuminating the intimate relationship of the Appalachian hillfolk with the land and ancestors and getting back to the root of the Appalachian folk-magic tradition.
-Denise Alvarado, author of the *Voodoo Hoodoo Spellbook*

It's been a very long time since a new book on any aspect of contemporary paganism came along that has not only seemed worthwhile but impressive. Byron Ballard's fascinating, engaging new book on Appalachian hoodoo beliefs and practices is not only a sparkling treasure chest of folklore and magical tidbits, it is full of pragmatic and wise advice on how to think, live, and thrive in a changing world. Not for the faint of heart, this book will teach you how to hex, and also how to heal. It'll explain to you things you know (growing your own food is a good idea and fun) and things you don't (did you know you can expose a liar in public with very little effort?) and things you never thought you'd think about (I'll let you find out for yourself). Ballard is a charming writer, and this book brings her sly wit, native intelligence, and sense of community compassion to any reader lucky enough to procure a copy. I can't imagine not having this book in my library or not wanting to gift it to many friends.

-Peg Aloi, Media Coordinator,
The Witches' Voice; creator of
"The Witching Hour" blog;
media scholar; film critic; author

CONTENTS

INTRODUCTION

Before we get too far down this road, I think you all should know about the process that got me to teaching workshops on Appalachian folk magic and, now, to writing about it. In 2006, I presented a paper at Harvard, at a colloquium titled "Forging Folklore: Witches, Pagans, and Neo-Tribal Cultures." It was organized by Hannah Johnston and Peg Aloi, and I was booked in as an independent scholar. The paper is about my journey out of and then back into my deep Appalachian roots. It's the same journey many people make as they age—they leave the past behind and then come back to embrace the parts of it that still have grace and power. And love, of course. That's a big part of all of it.

That paper—called "Hillfolk Hoodoo and the Question of Cultural Strip-mining"—was later published in Women's Voices in Magic (Megalithica Books, edited by Brandy Williams) and featured in the premiere edition of Hoodoo & Conjure Quarterly as part of a longer essay called "Cove-Witches & Curanderas." You'll find it at the end of the Introduction.

People get confused when they meet me because I don't have a strong regional accent. I also practice a minority religion that usually brands me as a kook from California. And I wear shoes, even in the summer. I do have bad teeth, though, in spite of the best efforts of a wonderful periodontist, so that part of the hillbilly stereotype holds. I think if I reach the age of sixty, I'll take up smoking a corncob pipe.

When I attended that folklore conference at Harvard, I spent a glorious, heady weekend with other bright people who presented papers in their chosen fields. And in the irony department, I stayed at a bed-and-breakfast that was in a house previously owned by Al Capp, of Lil Abner fame.

After much thought and conversations with a wide range of people, I decided to share some of this information. I found that there is a hunger in both the dominant culture and in my spiritual community for authentic information on this subject. My spiritual community is also yearning for workings that, well, that work. I did some research, talked to some home-folks, and created a series of workshops based on what I have learned and practiced over the years. The five workshops are: "Hillfolks Hoodoo for Beginners and Outlanders," "Hillfolks Hoodoo Intensive—Body Parts and Eggs," "Reading Signs and Omens," "Becoming the Oracle—an Introduction to Divination," and "Hillfolks' Hoodoo Intensive—Cartomancy." I've bundled the five together in a set that gives the student a good overview of techniques, history, and a glimpse into the culture from which they all flowed.

This book encompasses all that information and includes some essays I've written over the years about my southern Highlands culture. I've included them in the book because there are still too many "hillbilly" jokes and too many cultural stereotypes that seem impossible to remove from the surrounding culture's perception of Appalachian people. The cultures of the mountains are certainly fading, and some parts of it are easy to shed, to be perfectly honest. There are, however, plenty of people coming into the area, and they are learning from some of the older techniques of resourcefulness—how to preserve food for the winter, how to grow the kinds of crops that are nourishing and will keep well, the importance of livestock to a small holding.

They are learning, in short, how to be subsistence farmers. It sounds peculiar when we think of it that way, but living close to the land and learning the ways of the particular microclimate in which you live are invaluable. As the larger culture begins to fracture, local people are left to help each other, to eat local food, to relocalize every part of their lives as the era of cheap petroleum comes to its screeching end.

Instead of reinventing those particular wheels, we can look to how the indigenous peoples—both American Indian and long-migrated Europeans— survived in a land that was hard. In general, the land here is too hilly and soil poor for deep farming, too remote for ease of access to markets—the resources must be managed carefully, and the yield is dependent on the earnestness with which the land is tended and renewed at each season.

We read old manuals and we talk to old farmers and we try to ken what it is they really know. Here it is, the big silver bullet of Appalachian farming—you have to know your piece of land. You have to observe the patterns of wind and rain, you need to prepare for winter even if—in this age of warming—it never comes.

You have to glean out the kernels of predictableness in these mountains of unpredictability.

Knowing the land, knowing the microclimate that is your growing area and knowing your neighbors have saved many a family, going back as far as when this land was settled. The first time.

So kick back a little and join me for an exploration, a ramble through these quaint and interesting and necessary techniques. You may not end up as a bona fide mountain cove doctor, but I am hopeful you'll end up with enough knowledge to have some respect for this old and receding culture that I call the southern Highlands of Appalachia.

Here's that original piece:

Hillfolk Hoodoo and the Question of Cultural Strip-mining

When I was a child, my family lived in a small house at the head of a cove in western North Carolina. My mother was from a city family, but my father's family were only recent city dwellers so that when my father was looking for a place to live after the Second World War, he chose a place in the country. The property consisted of a few hilly acres of woodland, a grape arbor and apple orchard, and a house with running water in the kitchen but no indoor bathroom. My father bought the house from the people who lived down the cove from us—they had built another house, nearer the spring, and decided to sell the piece of property at the top of the hill because there was not enough water there. I left the home place when

I was eighteen and went to college and afterward to graduate school. In spite of my education and lack of accent, make no mistake about it—I am a redneck girl. I am your worst nightmare—as a country music song goes—an "educated redneck" (Jerry Lee Surber: Hey... Guitar). My family said I had "the big head" and the phrase "she's got above her raising" has been used, with some regularity, to describe my peculiar behavior.

I come from a family of Appalachian witches, at least on my mother's side. My grandmother self-identified and was identified by friends and fellow choir members as a witch. She had precognitive dreams and seemed to know things before they happened. She had a special warning dream that she never told anyone the specifics of, and when she called you to say she'd had The Dream, you paid attention because her dreams were never wrong. This strain of witchcraft runs back several generations in our family oral history, but no one lists witchcraft on census forms, so Ancestry.com is no help in my quest to find out how far back the Westmoreland women were considered witches. It seems to fall along the English branch of the family, the Irish branch given only to singing, drink, and bad temper.

I was told that I would get a "gift" when I grew up, a family gift, like my grandmother's dreams or my great-grandmother's healing power. My mother always thought the gift had skipped her, but she was obsessed with ghosts when I was young and we would go ghost hunting sometimes on the weekends, bundling up in the old pink Buick to drive to some place my mother had heard was haunted. The home place had the ghost of the old man who built it—Mr. Haney—who would clear his throat outside in the yard, early in the morning. And my mother's parents moved into a house in the city in an older neighborhood where the ghost in residence was Mrs. Brown. Nowadays, we would say that my mother's gift was the ability to recognize discarnate spirits, but we didn't have fancy words for what we were and what we did. Some folks had the healing, some folks had the seeing, some could stop a flow of blood by reading a verse from the Bible. My mama liked spooks. It didn't seem weird or particularly unnatural—there were plenty of neighbors who also had abilities like that—we called them granny-women and cove doctors sometimes.

But mostly we called them Grammaw or Mz. Swanger or Old Lady Boyd. They knew a baby had to have a silver dime on a string around her neck to make it easy for teeth to cut through. They knew if you didn't give an infant catnip tea, then hives would break out on the inside and kill her. They knew about spring tonics and poultices, about what greens you could eat. I learned the burn spell from them, thought they didn't call it a spell. It was just the words you said if somebody had a bad burn, and then the burn got better. I learned healing techniques from those women, when and how to plant a garden, how to divine the weather and to read an ordinary deck of playing cards to see the future. It wasn't fancy. It didn't require a special outfit or special ritual tools. It is a down-home witchcraft that is simple and effective. Something that comes naturally and uses materials at hand. It is based on generations of living close to the land and being poor and making do.

We know from anthropological studies that witchcraft is cross-cultural and is the practice of peasant medicine and psychology. My family never saw witchcraft as their religion. They were Methodists— my great-grandfather was one of the founders of a Methodist church, and my grandmother's second husband was a lay minister. When I became ordained as a Wiccan high priestess just before my grandmother's death, she thought it was funny that I had joined the two family practices of witchcraft and preaching. She was, after all, the woman who said that God isn't some old man on a throne in the sky: God is energy, plain and simple. What my grandmother didn't realize was that I was also marrying the traditions of Appalachian witchcraft to the newish religion called Wicca. I am both a lower case and an upper case witch/Witch; I got a double dose of witching, an extra helping, as it were. And lately I've taken to calling what I learned and what I do hillfolks' hoodoo, with a nod toward those other hoodoos that are practiced around America. Kitchen witchery, some call it. But "hoodoo" suits me because a cousin once told me that our family could put "the hoodoo" on you. She seemed unnerved by it, but I always liked it. Putting on the hoodoo was like putting on the Ritz—a special talent reserved for folks like us. Hillfolks.

What is hillfolks' hoodoo—the kind that's practiced in the southern Highlands of Appalachia? It's medicine and midwifery; it's omen-reading and weather working. Sometimes it requires the witch to have a listening ear and an open heart: she may be asked to give advice or to keep a secret. It's working in both the physical realm and in the psychological one, using keen observation, common sense, experience and folkways to effect change.

When I entered college, it was the heady '70s and I was part of a women's encounter group that met in the student center and drank beer and created ritual. It was there I became a Wiccan, a religious Witch. And then I left it all alone as I pursued a career in theatre and arts management and grew older. Yes, I knew in advance that someone would try to assassinate Reagan and that he would live. And I knew when my paternal grandmother died, though no one told me for a week. But the old lore and practices weren't necessary in my urban modern world. Voice and diction classes lifted my native accent, and I was a city girl, living an artist's life.

When my daughter was born, I started thinking about the family gifts. Not long afterward, my grandmother died, and I began to feel a nagging urge to remember what I'd learned growing up redneck in west Buncombe County. I started practicing the old charms and salves and planting an urban garden by the right signs of the moon. It was good to remember, to claim my place in that lineage. Today I call myself "Asheville's Village Witch," and Asheville is mostly all right with that. My daughter doesn't even mind it—well, not too much.

My family has been in western North Carolina for a long time, and we are seeing staggering changes in the southern mountains of Appalachia. There are newcomers daily, building McMansions on the hilltops and gated communities of ugly condominiums on farmland that used to boast corn, tobacco, and sorghum. We used to call those folks flatlanders or flatland touristers or outlanders because they came from somewhere that wasn't here. Asheville has also become a New Age Mecca, the Sedona of the East, the Salem of the South and you can easily spend a thousand dollars to align your chakras or attend a weekend retreat with a famous speaker who will tell you the secret that will make your spiritual experiences have meaning or will fill your pockets with money. There are special metaphysical bookstores where one can buy a book or crystal or deck of tarot cards. The knowing that I experienced in the hollows of the mountains is being overlaid by something that feels less natural and more desperate than what we did in the cove. I was told a few years ago that I shouldn't call myself a witch because I didn't practice a British traditional witchcraft. The woman who said this wasn't from here; she was from off, of course—a sparkly young Gardnerian priestess with a proper lineage.

People come into the area with money to spare and a spiritual hunger that simply isn't slaked by reading the latest self-help book. They have left their birth religions for a thousand reasons, and they've sampled some Buddhism and tippled at Tantra and spoke Lakota during their spiritual ceremonies. They are neither Lakota nor Buddhist, but they are voracious, their hunger never appeased. They want a tribe and they have been separated from their tribal selves for so long that they don't even know where to look.

So they look to Africa and to the First Nations in North America. The Norwegian-Americans sport dreadlocks, the skinny white kids want tattoos and piercing, all in an effort to feel the connection of tribe, a connection more powerful and less intimate than family, a connection that remains even when a member is pulled from their tribal village.

I come from a kind of tribe, an old-fashioned neighborhood where everybody knew everybody's business and adults watched kids and corrected them with a switch, if necessary. It is an insular and claustrophobic way to live, certainly difficult if you don't fit into the dominant and dominating culture of your tribe. If you get above your raising, it is sometimes difficult to go home again, to fit comfortably into the tribal roles that have been assigned us since the beginnings of our tribal roots. My tribe are hillfolks, and we share some qualities with hillfolks in other parts of the country—the ones in Arkansas and in upstate New York. We see ourselves mocked at every turn as "hillbillies"—inbred, corn likker-swilling morons, proud of our lack of education and our xenophobia. We watched The Beverly Hillbillies when I was a kid, and we read Lil' Abner and Snuffy Smith. There were children that I knew who couldn't get their new shoes for the school year until the tobacco crop ("the burley") had been sold. My father was not a hardscrabble farmer. He was a truck driver. We didn't get new shoes very often either (at least not until my father joined the Teamsters), and we did go barefoot in the summer and we did catch crawdads in the creek. We ate green apples, and we went fishing at Jack

Hipps' fishing lake in the next cove over. So, in some ways, possibly in many ways, we fit the stereotype. I look back and think how grand it was to grow up feral on the side of a mountain, sneaking down the hill on Friday evenings to listen to hillbilly music played by real hillbillies at our neighbor's log cabin. I didn't realize until later that we were a laughable remnant of an America that will soon be lost to progress and assimilation. Good heavens, I am part of the last two demographics that America can still mock with impunity—I am a fat hillbilly.

Jeff Foxworthy has made his fame and fortune, mocking the people he comes from—bad form perhaps, but a lovely bit of self-interest. He is not the first, nor will he be the last. At least he comes out of the culture and isn't an outlander poking fun at our supposed lack of sophistication and our refusal to be like the rest of America. It is the rare commentator that "gets" us— most err on the side of "Cletus the Slack-Jawed Yokel" (Matt Groening. "The Simpsons"), a few make us sound like noble throwbacks to a quaint Shakespearean age. Often writers have come out of this culture and look back on it with a rosy romanticism that forgets the hardship of carrying water from the spring, of heating a house with paper-thin walls during a mountain winter, the relentless low-level stress of growing the food you eat and the cash crop that will pay your taxes. We are neither one nor the other but both. It has taken me some time to know this, but I am glad of the knowing.

I am also glad for the things I learned there. Because of women in those two coves—and in Benson Holler on the other side of the woods where my cousin Dena lived—I practice a kind of witchcraft that is natural and easy. When I am called on to help someone with a health issue or a relationship issue, I can brew up a cup of tea and talk it through. When I am called because someone feels their house is haunted, I load up a little basket of salt and grits and vervain and corn liquor and I head out the door to do some Appalachian feng shui. I have become the village witch for much of my community, and when I say "my community" I am not only talking about the Pagans and Wiccans who are my co-religionists, I am also talking about the regular folks in my neighborhood who feel like they need a change of luck or who want to know what kind of tincture they should take for hives. I have become an urban cove doctor, though I don't say wisewoman. That sounds like I got the big head.

Here in America, people tend to be spiritual seekers. And educated Americans tend to look in all sorts of places for the things they feel are missing in the religion they practiced growing up. They have adopted and adapted practices from the indigenous peoples around the world. My Cherokee friend MariJo Moore says she always shudders when she sees people driving around with dream catchers hanging from their rearview mirrors. You white people, she says with a shrug, will steal anything. They take "Indian names" so that a person called Rainbow White Feather is quite likely to have started life as Jennie Gardner and a person called Willard Junaluska is likely to be Cherokee and a Baptist. Confusing, I reckon.

We tribeless white people learn dances and songs from other cultures that seem deeply spiritual to us, though we don't know their context or deeper cultural meanings, we just like the way they look or sound or make us feel. We think they're cool. We figure if some tribal folks have been doing this for a long time, it must be good. And authentic. And more real than the last feel-good, self-help workshop or book or website we devoured in our hunger for a real spiritual experience, the kind we can't find in our tired old Protestant Christian churches. We love to go to interfaith gatherings and hear the call to prayer or learn a Dance of Universal Peace or make a small talisman. We love to hear those black church choirs, and we thrill to the sound of big African drums. They call to us, in a way that seems timeless. And we steal ideas of sweat lodges and vision quests from indigenous peoples and don't even know what the tribal affiliation is—we just say "Native American." We go to workshops by people who practice African traditions and we have some of that too. We bring rocks from home and a bit of bone from who knows where—because where do city people get bones? Kentucky Fried Chicken? Whole Foods organic markets?

We will dabble in anything that seems new or cool or more spiritual than the last thing, until we twirl and twirl and feel that we're so close to getting It, whatever It is—that missing piece that will give us Nirvana or Enlightenment or make us an Ascended Master. And we will pay dearly for rubbish and warmed-over religious hash because we don't want to slow down enough to dig in. Dig into our own traditions, dig into the earth, dig into our boring or hurtful family. We are rootless, alone, craving community and belonging. We must find our own tribes. But it requires work and confusion and dealing with loss on a massive scale. We white European-Americans had tribes once, a thousand years ago or more, tribes of woad-painted warriors with limed hair. We had drums and sweats and mystery. And we lost it and gave it away and let it be absorbed into other things, into folkways and fairy tales, until there was almost nothing left to reclaim, nothing left to honor. We colonized much of the planet only to find ourselves alone and pale, dreaming of firelight on wattle walls, aching for home.

Now we are turning our attentions to something that seems almost familiar to us, familiar in the same eerie way that the green-faced witch of Halloween is familiar. We have these insular mountain people in Appalachia, they think, these zany toothless hillbillies with their ignorant ways and ignorant-sounding accents. They are like us but also unlike us. They are clannish and separatist, from the same stock as the limed-haired warriors but gentled now, just as the fearsome ancient Danes are now the makers of sleek furniture and wedding cookies. They eat weeds right out of the yard and have the knowing of things unseen. They have mystery. They have hidden knowledge.

In the mountains, it's an old story. Each family has fewer children. Children leave home—and I mean really leave home—go to other states, other countries, choosing to relocate to better job markets or to live near the spouse's family. The old ways are not important in these new urban lives. We are self-conscious about granny healing, not sure if it's okay to be a cove woman. Outlanders buy up the farmland, drive up the taxes, make the landscape unfamiliar. And we are willing participants, selling the old home place for more money than we could ever have dreamed of.

But that leaves the question of this odd knowing, these healing modalities that aren't necessary in the modern world of western medicine, of Merck and Pfizer. It was easy to pass on the knowledge when there was a houseful of girls who would be responsible for doctoring animals and birthing babies. You picked the likeliest one, the one with the most talent for the work, and you taught her the charms, you showed her the roots and the herbs she'd need. No need to be sexist about all this—it could have been your son who showed the most promise, and so you taught him— though he would be unlikely, as a "cunning man" to practice midwifery. He'd do more weather work and divination, maybe some animal doctoring.

But those kids have left the farms and the hollers and are getting engineering degrees at Georgia Tech and work for Google and go to Atlanta to be rappers. And there are all those outlanders who seem sincere and want to learn what you learned from your grammaw. And they'll pay good money for it too.

So what's a mountain witch to do? I'm lucky to have a daughter who was raised Wiccan and wants to know what I know, what my foremothers knew. She seems to have gotten the gift my mother had—she sees ghosts and has great sympathy for their plight. When things go bump in the night on a winter evening, she shrugs and tells them to be quiet, she's trying to sleep. She plays around with a deck of tarot cards and has been known to do weather work to bring enough snow to close school on the day of that biology test she hasn't studied for. I did the same when I was young.

But not every witch is so lucky. What if there's no one left in the family who wants this folk-healing knowledge? Should it pass from the culture in the same way a recipe or a family story is lost? One answer is to pass the lore on to another generation who has interest in it. People who have come into the mountains from elsewhere. Outlanders.

People from other places think they are "practically a native" if they've been in the area for five years, but hillfolks don't see it that way. There's a saying in the mountains that you're not from here unless your granddaddy was from here. When you have little—a few stony acres and a tobacco allotment—pride of place can run surprisingly deep. It's the feeling of being tied to a particular piece of land, whether it's your family home place or the long range of the Blue Ridge itself. I say I have deep and gnarly roots in western North Carolina.

I can sit on the porch of the Grove Park Inn and see the mountain that shelters the cove of my raising, the general vicinity of where I went to school, the mill village where five generations of my family lived and died, and even the hill upon which my Westmoreland family is buried. It was stunning to sit on the wide porch of the Inn, high above the city, discussing the Theosophical Society with a new acquaintance, complaining about the rigors of air travel in this new age of heightened security and realize that almost my whole life was laid out in the hills and valleys below me.

I am a native. I am of a particular place, and in a way that is difficult to define, I belong there. This knowledge I have is imbedded in this culture and the culture itself is thinning, as more and more people assimilate into the dominant culture. But here come those hungry outlanders, those people who need a spiritual tribe to belong to. They are not my tribe, are they? They are not respectful of my culture—not hesitating to correct my pronunciation of common words or tell me funny hillbilly stories. They come here to suck up what they find appealing about the culture and to let the rest fall away or die beneath the wheels of modern progress.

Mountain philosopher and storyteller Marilyn McMinn-McCredie refers to this as "cultural strip-mining" because the culture itself gains nothing from the exchange and in fact yields up precious material that leaves the culture weaker than before. She likens it to mountaintop removal and to clear-cutting, which gut the area of natural resources and leave an ecological disaster behind. Then the mining company or the timber company move on to the next mountain, the next forest, as though all resources are renewable, nothing lost in the destruction, and much profit gained.

Is this also true of culturally embedded practices, like witchcraft? Some people think so and believe the charms and portents of their grandparents' generation are best left here to thin out into obscurity and so to disappear from the mountains, to be lost. Those people feel that this knowledge should only belong to the people whose direct ancestors collected and retained it. In our typical land-proud and insular way, some think it's better to lose the knowledge than to pass it out into the larger world, a world that scorns everything about our culture, except this one thing that seems to have value for them.

Others think that the knowledge is too valuable, especially now as we face so many environmental challenges, to be lost forever. The kind of assimilation that comes of blending old learning with newer modalities has a remarkable ability to reach a large pool of potential talent, to bring this working into a new world and a new age, with new people. Justin Britt-Gibson, in a piece in the Washington Post expressed it this way: "...how far we've come since the days when people dressed, talked and celebrated only that which sprang from their own background. For the first time in my life, I (am) fully aware of the spiritual concept that we're all simply one."

Do we owe it to the rest of you to share this: Do we owe it to our ancestors to pass it on? Or is it best to let it die a decent death, quietly and with some dignity, than to see it packaged and mass-produced, the latest gimmick in the New Age spirituality machine, like dream catchers or vision quests or sweat lodges?

I don't know the answers yet, but I and my hillbilly colleagues are conscious about the questions. We're weighing the pros and cons. We'll know what's right. When the time comes.

1. "Hoodoo origin and Thoughts on Etymology & Dictionary Makers" by Bill Cassleman; quotes from Daniel Cassidy, founder of An Léann Éireannach, traces the word "hoodoo" to Irish; "uath dubh," "dark shape."

CHAPTER ONE

AN OLD DIRT ROAD: SEEKING A CRAFT WITH NO NAME

First off, I need you to know that if you go picking through the hollers and townships in western North Carolina looking for an elder who practices "hillfolks' hoodoo," you will be sadly disappointed. If you come to the wilds and coves of these old mountains and are looking for people who practice traditional Appalachian healing or folk magic, you will never find them by inquiring at the dusty convenience store—where do I find locals who practice this hillfolks' hoodoo? Likewise, if you come as an ethnographer looking for remnants of traditional Appalachian folk magic, you may never get a satisfactory answer.

This thing that some of us do—it really doesn't have a name. I call it "hillfolks' hoodoo" as a branding technique, because it is alliterative and because the general public has some sort of notion of what "hoodoo" is—though they are often incorrect in the notioning of it.

It is a technique for highlighting this set of skills in a way that begins to feel at least somewhat familiar to a modern audience. I don't like to use the word "hillbilly"; in fact, I don't like anyone to use it. So I've chosen "hillfolks." I could have used "mountaineers," but that implies people who climb mountains. I could have used "mountain folk," but I decided it was too long and not very user-friendly. So I've settled on "hillfolks," and I've added "hoodoo" because it is familiar to most people even if they don't understand it exactly.

There is a large and unruly family of folk practices that fall under the label "hoodoo." Most of it comes from the African diasporas and carries a strong flavor of Catholicism. These hoodoos are, generally speaking, folk-magic practices and are used for healing, for acquiring resources (including affection), or for justice in personal matters.

I tell my students that all their clients will want one of the following things—good health, change of luck, money, love, or revenge. When you know how simple our human needs really are, then you begin to acquire techniques, resources, and tools to make that possible.

Hillfolks' hoodoo comes out of the long and sometimes prickly interaction of the native Indian peoples and the Scots-Irish, Irish and German immigrants in these remote hills. The European immigrants who came here were generally attracted to the idea of being on their own, out of the spying eyes and interfering interest of close-by neighbors. They relished the freedom and faced the hardships head-on. Stubbornness was and is a healthy attribute in these mountains. And we are legendary for our pride in our self-reliance.

Life in those early years was hard, and in some areas life continues to be so. Mercifully, there aren't big veins of coal in these parts, so the closest many people came to that sort of ready resource was the timber industry. In the late nineteenth and early twentieth centuries, that industry stripped these old mountain ranges of their old-growth timber and gave a dangerous living to local people.

My immediate people were sometimes millworkers, sometimes storekeepers, sometimes retail clerks. They gardened but didn't really farm. They had chickens and sometimes a cow—though my illustrious Ancestor Belle Ballard had a dairy farm, and I learned how to milk a cow from my great uncle John, who kept a small herd and grew his own silage corn and clover for hay.

They were, for the most part, Protestants—either Methodist or Baptist—as were most of my neighbors in the cove where I grew up. The folk practices I use and adapt are not based on Catholic saints twinned to African deities. They are based in the old-time religion of harsh and beautiful Protestant cults, carried with them across the ocean from their equally harsh homelands.

In my work codifying the folk practices I know, I've written out and sometimes rethought and reworked the things I remember from my early years. I have also been gleaning useful techniques from other folk practices and the people who keep them alive in their communities and on the larger electronic community of the Internet. Some things I have borrowed—

"borried"—from those other traditions and found ways to incorporate them into my own practice.

The rootwork we are exploring in these pages is very much alive in the spirit-haunted landscape of the rural mountains, to paraphrase Flannery O'Connor. If you watched the antics of Granny on *The Beverly Hillbillies* as she scraped together poultices or insisted on spring tonics, you have a vague frame of reference for the work that is done by herb doctors throughout Appalachia. If you have doused for water with two wands and hope in your heart, you begin to see the scope of these practices. They have their beginnings in the conjure women and men of British history and folklore, in the practices compiled by Alexander Carmichael in the *Carmina Gaedelica*, in Cherokee houses and gardens, and in the need of poor and proud people in the fastnesses of the region.

TOOLS

We'll begin with the tools of the trade and will examine them in two separate sections. This first section holds the intellectual and esoteric keys to being a competent practitioner. The second section outlines some of the oddments that are carried in the baskets and bags of folks like me. It also includes an invitation for you to use your imagination to create the next generation of tools.

The Tools of Heart and Head

So much of what we do as rootworkers has to do with a deep understanding not only of technique but of clients, circumstances, and ourselves. These are skills that are polished with much use, remembering that practice makes perfect. Or at least pretty darned good.

The single most important thing you can master for this work—and also in life—is to be a good listener. When you yourself are quiet, you can attend to the sounds of life around you, you can hear what a client is saying underneath the actual words she uses, and you can hear the wee voice of intuition giving you further information.

Some people tend to chatter out of nervousness, and it's good to find ways to bring yourself to a grounded place. (There's a note about that in the Receipts section.) When you ground your energy, center yourself to a calm and open place and focus on the problem at hand, you will accomplish more than you can imagine. And it will be easier because you won't be fighting with yourself, fracturing your attention. Ground, center, focus.

My practice is not necessarily a religious one, but if you bring your spirituality into your work, you should add a prayer of thanks as you begin this listening process.

The next skill to set loose on this work is your own imagination. Some hoodoos rely on specific formulas for a particular working, and that is no bad thing. But with a free and easy imagination, you can discern new techniques for old problems, and you can also discover new tools and techniques suitable for new times and new issues.

A heightened attention to your native intuition is also a strong asset in this work. What is going on under the surface of the issue at hand? Are you detecting that your client is not giving you the full story? Your intuition works hand in hand with your keen imagination. With practice and experience, you will learn to trust your gut—it will be right more often than not.

When you have come to a listening, calm, and observant place, you will also begin to read the signs around you and to add that information to the work you do. If crows awakened you this morning, bring your interpretation of that into the work. The wind is coming from the east, with a smell of rain—this may be important in both your planting cycle and your workings for your clients and yourself.

There is a certain amount of showmanship that is required for this kind of work. There, I've said it. My early career was in the theatre, and I have found ways to utilize my training in the older work that I now do. And I must here thank the remarkable wordsmith Terry Pratchett for the concept of "boffo." Read his Tiffany Aching books, starting with *The Wee Free Men*. Especially handy when working with clients, boffo is the art of adding just enough flair to a working or reading to make it memorable, to make it stick in a client's mind. It is wearing a do-rag and a necklace of talismans when you make a public appearance. And it is certainly making good use of my favorite adage in this business—Attitude is Everything! Which leads us to the question of ethics.

These practices—what I think of as peasant medicine and psychology—are cross-cultural. Sometimes they are used in tandem with or absorbed by religious practice, and sometimes they are used full on, without an overlay of religion. I maintain they are always spiritual practices because your best work is done in concert with spirit beings who are your allies. (More on that later.)

Many of my students come from modern Wiccan or Pagan practice, and they are confused about what they can and can't do since many of them are bound by what is called the Three-Fold Law or the Law of Return. It is an idea that everything you put out into the Universe is returned to you three times over.

I have a quibble with that, as a matter of fact. I don't think that every little contrary thought comes back to smack you in the rear end. It is more the general attitude of the-world-is-against-me victimhood that hovers around and returns like a boomerang. It is the overall way you react with and in the world that sets those patterns.

Sometimes it goes back to the old adage of the half-filled glass—half-empty or half-full? It is the mindset of misfortune and misery that will cling to your soul like cockleburs if you let it. Optimist or pessimist will have more to do with what returns to you in this world than whether or not you had a bad thought about another human being.

Attitude is everything, and a generosity of spirit will go a long way toward keeping you grounded and sane and whole, which is the real meaning of healing.

That being said, don't call me up and ask me to magically kill your lawyer, as one client did. Lawsy, the things I've been asked to do.

Essay One

A Season of Lights: How We Celebrated a Hillbilly Yule

Like a lot of modern Pagans, I grew up celebrating a cultural Christmas that had less to do with Baby Jesus and more to do with bits and pieces of family practice that had become ingrained in the midwinter celebration over many generations. The earliest white settlers to this area brought with them a lot of traditions from the British Isles, and those traditions stayed in place for a long time in the isolated coves and towns in the western North Carolina mountains.

But I have found, in speaking with other natives and country folks that grew up about the time I did, that Appalachian "traditions" for Christmastime varied widely from family to family. They almost always included visiting neighbors and family and decorating an evergreen tree for the living room. Under this tree, Santa left gifts for the good and coal for the wicked, and most years, my brother and I got both.

Decorated trees weren't a common thing here until the Great Depression, but my fondest memories of the season revolve around the procuring of the tree, the general trauma of getting it into the house, and the subsequent endurance trial of its adornment. We were either too poor or too cheap or too stubborn to buy a tree, and we always went up on the mountain to cut one.

My father must have done it when I was very small, but it soon fell to me and my brother to clamber up the hill and find a good tree. It was always too tall, and we would cry and my dad would cuss as he trimmed it. My mother would supervise the decorating and grow progressively acrimonious.

There was an order to it, you see, and we never remembered, or if we did, we willfully ignored it. Putting the lights on was first, and that was a man's job. Then garland strands and plastic ornaments, saving the delicate glass ones until everyone was in a state of anxiety and agitation. The final touch was the icicles, which had to be tossed onto the tree, one by one, never hurled in shining clumps. We aimed for the top of the tree where sat, not a star, but a misshapen red glass bauble that looked for all the world like a Christmas robot.

It was excruciating.

It used to snow here in the mountains, which seems hard to believe in this era of too-warm and too-dry winters. Once there was a thick layer of perfect snow on the ground, and I had the bright idea of taking a hatchet and my brother and our Shetland pony up the mountain to bring home the tree. As a parent, I look back on this scenario with bewilderment, trying to imagine a mother who would blithely allow such an adventure.

Off we went and we did return with a tree. The pony flatly refused to have it tied to him, my brother was crying from the cold, and I ended up dragging the tree with one hand and the pony with the other, while screeching at my brother to stop crying and pick up the hatchet.

Again, the tree was too big. My mother yelled at us, and my brother cried some more, and I took the pony up to the shed. I refused to decorate it that year, busying myself by setting up the weird nativity scene on the bookshelf. It had the standard barn-shaped box that held some figurines that had come from my mother's side of the family.

One of the Wise Men looked like he was dipping snuff, and Joseph had never been in the picture. Mary and the manger had the place of honor, surrounded by sheep and cows and Wise Men. The kneeling shepherds lurked outside the box, where they were joined by dinosaurs, a fire truck, model horses and cars and, later, those small naked trolls with bright hair. The camels were beautifully appointed, and I always set them apart from the others so that their elegance was not marred by the shabby and cockeyed shepherds.

We always woke too early on Christmas morning and made a lot of noise until my parents were up too. They drank Bloody Marys, and we ate fudge and chocolate-covered cherries and played with our toys and broke them and then got dressed to visit my mother's parents. The day always ended in too much food and too much drink, in bad tempers and disappointment. The animals never knelt in our barn on Christmas eve, and we never had those glorious bubble lights on our tree, like the neighbors down the hill did.

Now years later, I approach the Winter Solstice with a sense of joy and relief. The tree always fits in the house, there's never any yelling, and we even have some bubble lights. I can hurl great masses of plastic icicles anywhere I want, and the tree is topped by a fairy, who beams down on our relative sanity in this most stressful time. In the early afternoon, we go over to my brother's house and see the niece and nephews, and we eat chocolate-covered cherries.

The only thing I really miss is the pony.

CHAPTER TWO

A LITTLE BIT FARTHER DOWN THE ROAD: TOOLS YOU CARRY IN A WORK-BASKET

There's a bit of naming we need to go over at this point. Some of you are familiar with the following ideas, but in the mountains they have a different name. I don't borry the more familiar ones, so you'll need to brush up on your English here. I'm putting a short but handy Glossary in the back of the book, for easy reference.

You may know about mojo or talisman bags or medicine bags, fine and useful tools from some African and American Indian traditions. We have something similar here, but we call them sachets. It is not pronounced in the French fashion as sashay but is pronounced sashet. In some mountain herbal medicine, you may wear a bag of certain herbs around your neck to affect healing, but generally sachets are folded small and stuck in a pocket.

They are usually made from brown paper or from newspaper. When I was a kid, they were sometimes folded from the same catalogues that graced the outhouse. I tie them with either binding twine or yarn, depending on the application.

"Voodoo dolls" are all the rage. Have you seen the little kits you can buy at your local bookstore? A poppet, to give it its old English name, is an effective tool in rootwork, and many cultures have them. Up here, we call them dollies, and they are made from almost any useable found material—rags, fabric scraps, corn shucks or large leaves. They are often filled with herbs or minerals for the desired outcome.

A written formula for a working is called a receipt, the old-fashioned word for recipe. Both words come from the Latin *recipere*, which means to take. In fact, the Rx for a prescription (take two and call me in the morning) comes from that word too. Women's housekeeping journals from times past often hold both recipes for delicious things to eat and recipes for healing techniques. (For more on archaic words, please visit Michael Quinion's excellent website World Wide Words at www.worldwidewords.org).

Now, onto the tools.

One of the things to remember about this kind of work is that your materials should be readily and cheaply available and close at hand. The people who originally practiced these hoodoo techniques didn't spend money—which they mostly didn't have—on costly store-bought charms or candles. They made do with what they had. Since they were mostly rural people, they had the vast resources of one of the most species-diverse places in the world.

CONTAINERS

Let's start with containers. I will sing you now a song of praise for the mighty Mason jar. It is familiar as a container for jams and jellies, but its uses are many, which is why it comes in so many sizes. Imminently reusable, strong, sturdy, user-friendly, the canning jar is indispensable in the work I do.

But you needn't invest in jars if you're not picky about having a uniform look on your workbench. Save your recycled jars and lids, or if the lids are unusable you may be able to find canning lids and rings that will fit. Junk stores will often have odd collections of canning jars, sometimes left there when the grandchildren have cleared out the deceased grandmother's basement or pantry. The lids and rings are easily acquired at a local hardware or grocery store, depending on your location.

I also use throwaway jars—the ones you or your neighbors recycle. Baby food jars are a good size but often don't reseal very well. Quart-sized plastic mayonnaise jars are readily available and close down tightly. There are some nicely-shaped jars that hold jams and jellies—I use them as long as the lid will screw down tightly and there are no stains on the inside of the lid. The heavy plastic ziplock bag is excellent for holding and storing fresh and dried herbs. Lightweight and easily portable, your tool basket can hold many different herbs and specimens in the various sizes of reclosable plastic bags. When you are harvesting herbs and other botanicals for your use or that of your clients, you may need to find ways to dry them for future use. Hanging them upside down is a pretty decoration in the kitchen, but a more traditional approach is to lay them out on a clean cloth or on newspaper in the rear window of your car. Your car will be nicely scented, insects won't disturb the drying process, and the drying will be accomplished fairly quickly. If you have the space, those wooden folding drying racks for clothes can also be used effectively.

CUTTING AND GRINDING TOOLS

Some of your materials can be cut up into smaller pieces with a sharp knife or with scissors. One of my favorite garden tools is a keen pair of secateurs—they deadhead the roses and also cut back the *Melissa officinalis*. A few sturdy, heavy and sharp knives are indispensable, and you'll need a cutting board as well. I have a cover in durable plastic that protects my cutting board from the vagaries of my herbal choices—I manage to get all the belladonna off the knife with a thorough application of soap and hot water.

Some materials need to be ground up though, and a mortar and pestle is my choice for that. I'd like to get one of those stone querns that you sometimes find in Mexican *tiendas*—they are called *molcajete*. Or one of those flat grinders called a *metate*... but for now my old brass mortar does an excellent job. Depending on how fine a chop you want, you could also invest in a secondhand blender and keep it separate from the one you use for cooking... or margaritas.

SMOKE TOOLS

We are familiar with the ceremonial pipe used by some American Indian tribes—of its ritual and cultural significance. Most modern Pagans also use particular kinds of smoke as a purification element when preparing for ritual or workings. White sage and cedar are commonly used in the Southwest, and that technique has become near ubiquitous when entering sacred space for ritual. Tobacco is used ceremonially—both as smoke and as an offering.

Appalachian practitioners also use tobacco, smudge, rabbit tobacco (*Gnaphalium obtusifolium*), apple wood—a variety of smokes for a variety of applications. Years ago, I saw an old cast-iron bean pot in the window of a local thrift store—too rusty to use (plus paint smears), but it makes the perfect cauldron for smoke work. It is deep and heavy so it doesn't get overheated, and the burning materials you put in the bottom are unlikely to blow out. Some other hoodoo and medicine traditions use a feather bundle or wing to waft the smoke, but I usually just use my hand. Another handy thing, though, are those funeral home fans that used to be found in every little Pentecostal church in the mountains. Stiff cardboard and a wooden handle make it a handy tool for wafting.

My big discovery a few years ago came from my stint as a beekeeper. Word to the wise—beekeeping is a noble and necessary art. If you are at all interested, I highly recommend it. Contact your local agricultural extension agency for information on bee groups in your area. One of a beekeeper's best tools is a smoker. You burn pine needles, dried herbs, etc. in a small bellows, and you puff the smoke over the hive you're working on. It keeps them calm and gives you a chance to work without too much aggravation from the dear golden critters.

You see where this is going, of course. We were doing a big ritual, and I decided to smudge folks with the bee smoker. It lays in a cool, intense cloud of smoke that is perfect for purifying a big group. I've since used it when doing energy clearings and before a big house blessing. No more fiddling around with a smudge stick, a big shell, and some feathers for me.

That takes us to the notion of cultural appropriation. Most modern Pagans use white sage to do smudging in an American Indian tribal style. I like sage—I think it has a clean smell. But as an Appalachian woman, I needed a smell that hints at the rich mixture of things that make up being a mountain woman. I'm developing my own purifying smoke that includes mountain mint, rabbit tobacco, dried witch hazel, and chips of apple wood. This year, I've also harvested some kudgy-vine flowers and I'm drying them to see if that sweet smell remains when burned. I'll let you know.

FIRE TOOLS

There are lots of fire tools, of course. Making fire can be done with those lovely strike-anywhere matches, though they are hard to find. I mostly use a fire stick—one of those long lighters that work so well with seven-day candles. I have flint and steel and one day am going to make new fire, just for fun. It's a skill I think more people should possess, don't you?

You'll also need some tools for illumination, and those will depend on exactly what you're illuminating. Sometimes a miner's light would be handy, shining right from the top of your forehead—when you have your hands full and are nudging a nosy dog with your knee. Usually a good strong flashlight is all you need. I prefer one of those battery-less ones that you either shake or pump up. I have one shaped like a little black cat that was given to me by my grad school roommate. An oil lamp can be evocative for readings or workings, and be sure to get plain oil, not scented.

Many hoodoo folks use candles for a variety of useful things. I like those plain seven-day candles (sometimes people call them "glass jar candles"). They burn safely and bright, and they can be anointed with oils and herbs. You can do a spell for someone and create a beautiful collage of images that is glued right onto the outside of one of those candles. When the candle is all burned down, the working is complete.

Though they are technically not fire, I also love battery-operated tea lights. Readily available in craft and discount stores, these little lights are good for a variety of uses, and they are perfectly safe. If you are setting up a little healing altar at a hospital or hospice, the battery tea light is your go-to candle. Likewise good for houses with small children, curious cats, or careless domestic partners, it's smart to have a supply of them on hand. The "Energy Trap" receipt you'll find at the back of this book makes good use of those little lights.

Your Allies—you really aren't ever alone

When engaging in any earth-based energy work, it is wise to remember that you don't have to work alone and you mostly shouldn't. There are many allies with whom you can cultivate a strong relationship and who can be helpful in time of need. We'll outline working with three different types here—The Cousins, the Ancestors and the Dead, and other root doctors.

I love to start with the Cousins—the name I use for the spirits of the land in which I and my people have lived for a long time. Land spirits are tricksters by nature, but they are also good-hearted (for the most part), and if you love and honor them, if you treat them right, they will have your back when you're working in the land.

My tradition includes a strong working relationship with those spirits of the land on which we dwell. I am careful to seek their advice and bring them their little treats. This relationship was forged on the mountain where I lived as a child, where I often communed with those cheerful but mischievous critters. They are valuable teachers and allies, useful and entertaining.

Before I start any working—whether a high-powered hex or a simple house blessing, I go out onto the land and leave offerings for the spirits of that place. I may be working in a neighboring county or on land with which I'm not familiar, so I strive to develop at least a respectful working relationship with the energies of that land.

I take a digging tool out into the yard (and if there isn't a yard, which is rare here, I leave the offering just outside the building), and I dig a wee hole. Into that I put some brightly colored cheap candy, the weirder the better. Gummy hamburgers—they love them. Mike and Ike's—those too. Cinnamon red-hots are good, as is candy corn. I bury it because most people don't want their dogs or kids eating that crap, but if they don't have dogs or kids (or don't care), I leave the offerings on the land.

Then I pour out a little alcohol, preferably corn liquor. That is dear sometimes, though, so any drink will do—whiskey, beer, that bad wine you couldn't finish. If you are in recovery or are a nondrinker, then I recommend sweet tea, the sweeter the better. Coffee can be offered too—very sweet, with cream.

Something shiny always comes next. You can use small pieces of broken glass or those glass beads that florists use. If you have access to mica, I'd use that. Natural and reflective, mica is a thoughtful choice to honor the spirits of your land. I also give them spent shotgun shells when I find them.

The next group of spirits is those beings that used to be living people. Your people. If you live in the place where your people settled, you may already be tending their graves and decorating their headstones at holy times. If that is the case, you can begin to familiarize yourself with their stories and form a relationship with them.

You might start with an Ancestor altar in your home or yard. Gather objects that either belonged to your people or remind you of them and set up a little display. Add photos if you have them. Leave a little dish of something you know they'd like—corn bread maybe.

In all probability, you don't live anywhere near The Old Home Place. But your mom has passed or your beloved grandpa. They will be with you no matter where you are. Set up a photo and some personal objects, and honor your connection with them. When you're in a jam, call on them. Sit in gratitude for what they sacrificed for you (if they did), and remember that you wouldn't be here, reading this book, without them.

You don't need to know their names. If you are adopted, you can use the ancestors in your adoptive family's line and you can also call on your bloodline. If you don't know the names, it might help you to think of them as your mother's mother, for instance.

There is a Museum of Appalachia north of Knoxville, Tennessee that has some weird and wonderful artifacts from the various cultures that came to be known as the Appalachian people. There is a whole room full of musical instruments made of found objects—a banjo made of a canned ham can comes to mind.

The museum—which is an associate of the Smithsonian—is well worth a visit. There's one section upstairs in the main building that has a horse-drawn hearse and several coffins. Several "angel crowns" are displayed too. Angel crowns are twisted rings of pillow feathers that come from the inside of a pillow used by a child that has died. This is a reminder to us that, in Appalachia and in other hard places, sometimes the Dead we honor are not our Ancestors but our Descendants.

The last group of allies we'll address here are the folks who practice what you practice. They can sometimes be tricky to find, but if you practice in your community, you will sooner or later catch up with them, or they with you. Folk-magic practices are part of every culture, but they are more secret in some places than in others.

Check to see who else has a "shingle" out in your town. If there is a metaphysical or occult store, those are often good places to check out. You'll need to keep your wits about you and not be taken in by some outlander who has come to make a buck off the gullible. Let your gut be your guide. If someone seems like a big drama-expelling charlatan, they probably are. You won't learn anything there, and that person might make use of you and your ability to shore up their own loose credentials.

We have new immigrants from the many lands south of our border, and they bring some interesting techniques with them, the *brujas* and the *curanderas*. I haven't met any here in my neck of the woods, but I suspect they keep a very low profile.

Tribal practices of American Indian tribes in your area are also similar to the rootwork we're talking about here. I recently met an herbalist and healer who is mostly Cherokee. We compared notes and talked about people we both knew out on Qualla Boundary. As I spend more time with my own mountain culture, I find it has just about anything a rootworker needs.

The Gullah people in the Low Country sea islands of South Carolina are also approachable and very knowledgeable. That is a beautiful African diaspora tradition that is wedded into Protestant Christian practices. And the food is very, very good.

I do have a dream of one day bringing together all those folk-magic practitioners in these southern Highlands and all of us bring our stuff and have a meal together and talk. No agenda, just sharing experiences and thoughts about the work. One day, maybe.

As with any ally, corporeal or noncorporeal, the thing you want to do is establish a relationship. You aren't swanning in to pick their brains and get their good stuff.

You are there to share what you know, to compare notes, to learn in a way that is humble and respectful. That goes across the board for anyone you encounter in this work. Don't be a jerk. Don't be a cultural stripminer. You are looking to work with spirits, with the Dead, with people who need your skills and abilities.

It's worth repeating in our hungry modern culture—don't be a jerk.

Essay Two

A Road to Somewhere

This essay may be too little, too late. Or as my dad would've said—a day late and a dollar short. But I want to explain, if I can, how we feel about our ancestors around here. I can sit on the porch of the Grove Park Inn and see the mountain that shelters the cove of my raising, the general place where I went to school, the mill village where five generations of my family lived and died, and the hill upon which my mother's family is buried. On birthdays, at Yuletide, on Decoration Day and at other times, I go to that hill and sit with my forebears.

The unnamed baby that died too young, the great-aunt who died in the "Spanish" Influenza of 1916, my great-grandmother, my grandmother, my mother—all reside now in this little piece of land that my family has "owned" for over a century. When I drive to the grocery store, my road takes me past the cool green place that holds the remains of my kindred. I remember them often, in little ways. And on important occasions, I bring flowers and food for them and sit on the ground remembering them, even the ones I never knew. They are my blood relations, my kin, my family.

Because I am from here, it isn't just the one burial place. I have relatives in a roadside cemetery near the old homeplace under Enka Lake and another branch of the family interred behind a church down near the airport. I don't visit those places as often, not more than a couple of times a year.

When the controversy over the "Road to Nowhere" began to claim a place in the public consciousness, it seemed far removed from me and mine. I was disturbed by the idea of "nowhere" because it seemed to me that the final resting place of one's family is somewhere, certainly a destination for the descendants on those holidays of remembrance that are still actively celebrated in the South and here in the southern mountains of Appalachia. And then it began to nag me as a symptom of a larger problem.

We live in a multicultural world and have since before that was a word in common usage. The cultural backdrop of the cove where I grew up is somewhat different than the backdrop of the folks over in Swain County. Urban cultures are different from suburban and rural ones. European-American and African-American and American Indian cultures are different and we struggle to understand each other. Visiting and tending the graves of your relatives is a cultural thing for the hillfolk in this area: culturally embedded and important to a way of life that is disappearing under the pressures of outside development and influences. No amount of monetary compensation for Swain County will ease the pain of this loss, not for the citizens whose people are buried there.

Don't get me wrong. I am as rabid an environmentalist as you're likely to find. I don't want roads cut through pristine forests; I am sickened by steep slope development and mountaintop clearing so that rich people can have a third or fourth vacation home.

But if families were told that a road would be built to give them access to the graves of their loved ones, then a road should be built. Not a four-lane boulevard with traffic lights and curbs—just a simple country lane that gets scraped a couple of times a year. I grew up on a road like that—many folks around here did. It won't be easy to build because the mountains make road building a challenge. But it should be built—as an increasingly rare act of good faith.

Like me, those folks don't just have one place to visit and tend—a completed road will give access to thirty-three cemeteries, the cool green resting places of people who lived and died in real communities. But the Federal government has broken promises about land before now—just ask the Cherokee.

CHAPTER THREE

AT THE CROSSROADS: MATERIALS

You can do much of this work by eliciting the help of your allies and using your intuition, but sometimes you need to lay in some supplies. I get supplies in several places—I grow some of what I need, I buy what I may need in markets and *botanicas*, and I barter with other rootworkers and practitioners for things I don't usually make and can't easily buy.

Let's start with that first notion—growing your own.

My workaday world includes whipping up anointed candles and wrapping helpful sachets with red string for clients. The Village Witch is not simply a handy marketing tool—we live in the last house on the left, near the river, and people contact me most days to do a little job of work for them, some paid, some bartered. There's a ragged old workbench on my front porch— the kind that is sometimes called a Welsh dresser—and

27

I also do a fair amount of work in my big kitchen. I grow all manner of herbs in the backyard, tucked between the vegetables, under the apple trees. There are so many places to order materials online, and students often want to know which source is "best." I encourage all of you to do your concocting and compounding at your own workbench. In our DIY world of Saturday morning runs to the local hardware store, why shouldn't you have the option of the old-school joy of doing it yourself?

I believe—a belief that comes of experience—that plants that grow where you live are the best ones to use. Here in the southern Highlands, we are blessed with an extraordinary variety of weeds and trees, many of them free for the gathering. My unmowed yard will yield the following wild green things, all of which I use in various degrees in different receipts: chickweed, violets, dead nettle, dandelion, creasy greens, Star of Bethlehem, blackberries, wine berries and kudzu. Since I'm a gardener, I've also planted lots of useful green friends—elderberry, raspberry, woad, vervain, rose, rosemary, sage, various mints (including wild mountain mint, *Pycnanthemum muticum*), hops, hellebores, witch hazel and many more. Trees include oak, apple, hawthorn, mulberry, cherry, maple, and locust.

Herbs from where you live and herbs you grow have several advantages. If you grow it, you know the soil, the land spirits, when it was harvested, how the plant was tended. If you are wise, you asked permission of the plant as you harvested and you honored the essence of this living being that is giving up its life to further your work.

A second advantage is the economic one—you can often get these plants for little or no money. We have several groups in our area that do plant swaps at the appropriate time of the year. That's where I've gotten many of my perennial herbs. Those herbs are very weedy, and if you grow them, you will find yourself looking for good homes for the babies, year after year. My garden boasts a beautiful bed of woad—*Isatis tinctoria*—that began as a single self-seeding biennial that left quite a lot of progeny behind it. I gave some of it away this spring, but now it is setting those curling and vivid blossom clusters. Which means, I'll be looking for homes for seedlings at the end of next season. This is true for the mint families—catnip, spearmint, and peppermint—as well as Melissa (lemon balm) and horehound. You'll be able to harvest all you need for your personal use and then trade, sell or give away the bounty of the garden.

A third advantage is saving time and gas. When you need something, you may very well be able to walk out your back door, pick a big handful of the appropriate green ally, and then come back in the house and use it immediately. Fresh and easily obtained—how nice to go from the garden to the workbench in a single walk through your yard.

As we explored in the previous chapter, the container of choice around these parts is the beautifully simple and readily available canning jar. Those jars come from several companies—Ball/Mason and Kerr are the most common. They range in size from quilted four ounces to pint to quart jars—I have even seen a gallon-sized one. I invest in a case of the half-gallon ones most years because they are so handy for tincturing a big batch of just about anything herby. I save various waters—ditchwater, melted hail and snow, stump water—in those same glass jars. Canning jars have long been used as freezer jars, too, and are very strong.

For oils, I pack the required herbs into a quart jar and fill it with either mineral oil or the cheapest vegetable oil I can find. I've had very good luck with infused rue oil made in this style. I am using more of that in my practice, for anointing candles and in sachets and other talismans. There's also a quart of woad oil infusing on my workbench right now.

Dry ingredients are easily stored in see-through glass jars, but it's best to keep them out of direct sunlight. I try to keep some jars and plastic bags with me, either in car or in bag, for those surprise finds along the way. A few seasons past, the ragged hedge near my daughter's school yielded a healthy amount of belladonna. Berries and all went into a zipper bag and then came home for drying.

With a supply of canning jars, backyard greens, a bottle of safflower oil, some help from your land spirits, and the good work of tending the soil of your land, you have a fascinating way to increase your supply cabinet. You don't have to be Martha Stewart to go from working the soil to working a receipt at your bench or table, all with materials you created yourself.

When you are looking to purchase your materials, go where the working people go. So many things are readily available—it is the very nature of this kind of work that the materials should be at hand. With all the Central American immigrants in our area, it's easy to walk into a bright *tienda* and find much of what you need. In fact, most of it is readily available in local grocery and hardware stores.

The last category is bartering or buying handmade products from your coworkers. I had the good fortune to live near a man who is a designer by trade but practiced traditional conjure as his hobby. He made some of the most beautiful compounds I have ever seen. His High John the Conqueror oil (John de Conker) was golden and perfect, bottled in a tall, heavy glass bottle and dressed with beads. There was some root in the mix too. It looked like—and was—the real deal.

He also came up with the idea of putting a plastic funnel in place of the lid on a Mason jar and screwing it in place with the jar's ring. It's an easy way to draw a line of redding or salt and works a treat for setting wards for clients.

If you have someone around who makes a beautiful product, please support them in their work. You will find that investment makes for a higher quality product, as well as a strong ally if you get in a jam.

Let's get down to it. Here are some very handy things that you will probably need if you get too much farther down this trail.

GREASES

These have a variety of applications in rootwork. Dressed with appropriate herbs and oils, they can be attached with a deft fingertip to almost any surface and will cling there until wiped away. Here in the mountains, lard and pork fats were readily available and still are. When I was growing up, my aunt Mary's husband Horace was a bear hunter. One family story involves Uncle Horace bringing my adorable wee self an uncured bear pelt, which I loved. Uncured, as you might imagine, meant that it got smelly and molty and no doubt maggoty and had to be gotten rid of. I was sad about it, so they tell me. It's hard to come by now, thank goodness, and must be refrigerated because it goes rancid quickly. Bear grease is very powerful—and also has a powerful smell.

Then there is the curiosity of "goose grease," which isn't made from goose fat at all. Into a greasy base—most now use beeswax and olive oil, but it could be any clean, rendered fat—you put in the classic ingredients for many healing ointments—menthol, camphor, wintergreen oils. Keep it tightly capped and in a cool place. Wonderful for healing, the old-timers used goose grease for almost any skin ailment.

Beeswax is used in many compounds. The best is from your own bees and includes honey and propolis. Low-melting temperature makes it easy to melt in a double boiler. I use beeswax for sealing jars of oils and waters. It gives a neat look to the packaging and adds its own strong properties to the work you're doing.

WATERS

This is one of the most varied categories in this section on materials. Workings in the mountains rely on many kinds of waters, all easily acquired. I've added a few borries to this—classic Florida water and Four Thieves vinegar. I use both in my energy work and find them to be very useful.

I cannot stress enough the importance of the use of water in this area of folk magic. Growing up, I heard stories about the uses of dishrags for various healing techniques—sopping-wet dishrags. They were buried in the garden or hung from a branch in the yard and allowed to dry. I used to wonder about the magic properties of those homely scraps of fabric—it took me many years to realize that the rag was merely the water-delivery system. The power was in the healing waters.

Waters hold an important place throughout world cultures, and we know that much of our body and our planet are composed of this living essence. Places where water flows upward from below-ground aquifers are considered sacred and magical: liminal places where the worlds of matter and spirit meet through the medium of water.

Different waters are used for different things, of course. Standing water—what I call ditchwater, though there are not so many ditches as there used to be when I was coming up—is particularly potent because it is water that no longer flows, water that has lost its ability to flow between the worlds. In addition, it has the added detritus of leaf, twig, mud and a generally unwholesome quality that is perfect for many kinds of workings. I personally love stump water because it is now so rare, but ditchwater is almost always my go-to water.

Here are some of the many uses of plain old water—and you will come up with some of your own as you get used to this. Always remember that once a water has been compounded in those ways it should not be ingested. It's good for jar talismans, anointing and such, but I don't want to hear about your drinking ditchwater, you hear me? Those cooling waters have a variety of applications. We'll list them here with brief, if occasionally redundant, definitions.

Fresh water—water from wells, springs and creeks. If you use tap water, leave it open to the air for a full day before compounding with it.

Bottled water from the store—you may choose to use a water from a particular locale for a particular working. There are some beautiful bottled waters called Celtic Water (bottled in France) that I sometimes use for workings. A bubbly water might be just the thing to add some vitality back into a person or situation. Unlike tap water, keep these waters tightly capped until ready for use.

Willow water—fresh water infused with willow leaves and stems. I make this in the early spring when the willows first leaf out. Use spring water, if you can get it—even if you buy bottled spring water at the grocery store. I often use collected rainwater. Let the leaves infuse in a cool place for a moon cycle, then decant.

Ditchwater—stagnant, muddy water from a ditch, not to put too fine a point on it. This is perfect for bindings, for holding information secret and for protection.

Stump water—rare in these days of stump grinders. It is rain water pooled in the depression in the middle of a stump. Perfect for healing—both physical and spiritual—this water holds the essence of the tree in which it steeped.

Dishwater—the tepid, greasy water that is left after you've done the dishes. No need to save this in a bottle—best to be mindful of needing it as you are doing the dishes. You can begin a working as you clean the glasses and will have it clear in your mind and ready for the last step as your scrub out the cast iron.

Lightning water—rainwater gathered during or after a lightning storm. I use it to add a charge to a working.

Snowmelt—melted snow. You'll need to replenish your stock at the first snowfall of the year. Assuming you have one. If there isn't snow in your part of the world, you can substitute other waters for this one.

Moon water—fresh water that is left out all night under a full moon. I use this for anointing people who are doing work in their dreams. Opens you to visions, keeps things soft.

Hail water—melted hailstones. May take a bit of bravery to gather this water—put on a thick hat and go out into a hailstorm with a Mason jar. Fill it 3/4 of the way full and allow the hail to melt.

Many hot waters are used medicinally and are made by steeping herbs, spices, or flowers in boiling water. These are teas and tisanes. Catnip and nettle are especially popular in the southern Highlands. Gargling hot water with the addition of salt is a sovereign remedy for sore throat and mouth ulcers.

Vinegar is used for a variety of things traditionally, and unfiltered apple cider vinegar is the liveliest and my personal favorite. It has both healing and magical proper ties.

Florida Water (*Agua de Florida*) is a lightly scented cologne and a borry, as I mentioned earlier. It is often used for blessings and for protection. I am currently developing a mountain version of this sweet water and will discontinue this borry once I'm satisfied with the results. In African diaspora traditions, this is also used as a draw and gift for the Ancestors and other spirit-folk, but mine don't like it. They prefer plain rosewater, which I make in the spring.

Blood and urine—nothing makes a working personal like the addition of some of your own bodily fluids. Spit, urine, and blood can be used for banishings, hexes, and other baneful workings.

Honey is used medicinally as a wound dressing and is used magically to attract and bind a working. Use local honey when you can. Have backyard bees if you are allowed and not allergic.

HERBS & ROOTS

This will be a slim section on an enormous topic because I am writing a series of articles on the uses of traditional mountain weeds that may become a book of its own. I present this brief list to you with some descriptions of use, knowing that I am giving you only a sip of spring water from this extensive dipper.

I make use of a wide variety of herbs and roots, and I use them in a variety of ways. Since I am talking about rootwork and not medicinal qualities, I will focus on those uses. In my community—as in yours, no doubt—there are well-trained and helpful herbalists who are my allies in the healing arts. Seek out those people in your neighborhood, find the good ones with accurate information, and give them some support, respect... and business.

Gathering these materials is easy, if you are growing them (or allowing them to grow) in your backyard on the edges of your garden. But if that isn't the case, here's some advice. First, don't go on someone else's property without permission. We're pretty picky up here about people tramping around over our land, so that's your word to the wise. And secondly—and this may sound silly to you—ask the plant's permission. To illustrate that, I'll share my witch hazel story.

In preparing to lead a Hillfolks' Hoodoo workshop, I was gazing out the window and observing the witch hazel in my front yard. It was wintertime, and the plant still held its dried leaves. It got me thinking about the properties of a plant that holds on to its old finery while preparing to bloom. Thinking it would be a good example for the workshop, I went outside to the plant to take a few leaves.

They would neither yield to tugging nor be broken off. My casual grab turned into a battle of wills, and I was ready to go into the house for the secateurs when I remembered my manners. I put my hands out, palms up, and asked if I might have a few leaves for the people to see. I then took a deep breath and reached out for the two leaves nearest me. They snapped free in my hand, and I had another illustration of how we should and should not interact in our world. I share it with you to remind you to have some respect for your materials and their sources and to always mind your manners.

I use roots in several ways. Sometimes they are dried and ground. Sometimes they are used chopped and fresh. I have immersed roots in oil or alcohol. I have hung roots from the fence to ward off various things. (That last technique does not work with groundhogs, by the way.)

Here are some of my personal favorites. They are the roots of powerful and successful weeds and are plentiful, at least for now.

Dock root—dock is a big, sturdy plant with a fat yellow root. Use it dried to aid in workings involving strengthening.

Kudzu root—I grew up calling this kudgey vine, and it is the bane of much of the southland. It's invasive, to say the least, and it sets an amazing root system. Dig deep after a period of gentle rain so that the ground is soft as far down as possible. Dig out the first set of roots and then follow the taproot down to the next level. You can keep digging down pretty far and not get all the root. Stop when you get tired. Use the young leaves for cooking and the root for workings you want to go fast.

Briar root (blackberry, raspberry, wineberry, even tame locust)—these are the common brambles at the edge of any cleared field. Use bramble root to add re-silience and toughness to a working. Blackberry jam is used to treat diarrhea, and chopped up briar root is used in sachets to add sweetness and tough beauty to a working.

Potatoes (Irish)—old-timers call these "arsh taters," and every mountain farmer grows them. In addition to good eating, they are also effective grated raw and used as a poultice on skin irritations.

Exposed tree root—when a large old tree falls over due to wind or weather, the exposed roots can be used in workings (to disable a seemingly strong adversary). Take a few shavings to use later.

Wild herbs—I grow most of these in my yard, and what I don't grow I gather from waste places like the edges of parking lots. There's a big patch of nettles by the river where I sometimes walk, and the city is hap-py for us to take all we want.

Nettles—for whipping a working into a frenzy.

Witch hazel—adds tough and mercurial qualities to a sachet. When you're creating a hex that needs to strike without warning. Witch hazel is the trickster herb in my personal botanica.

Oak—use all the bits: leaves, twigs, acorns. Oak gives substance and power and an indomitable will.

Mountain mint—you can smell this pennyroyal scent from yards away, and it grows fast. Use it in dream sachets to enliven dull dreams.

Catnip—the reverse action of mountain mint, cat-nip calms people, energies and situations.

Rabbit tobacco—make a sweet smoke for energy clearings and general cleansing.

Sumac—the flame-shaped clusters of berries work to bring your working into alignment with the energy of the place.

Vervain—not a wild one but one of my favorites. I use it as rocket fuel to kick-start almost any working.

Dusts and Dirts

I suppose it makes sense that an area with many different uses for water would also make use of dry compounds too. I use several dusts and dirts for compounding, for blowing into the wind, for sprinkling onto running water. As I did with the waters, here's a listing of some of them with a brief description where necessary.

Lavender powder—I prefer Yardley of London's because it comes in a pretty tin. I use it for soul puzzles and simple energy healings. Gentle but effective.

Dirt from your land/graveyard dirt—When clients worry that they can't focus, that they feel off-kilter or unbalanced, I advise them to put a pinch of dirt from their land in their pockets or in their shoes. My preference is for yard dirt, but even houseplant dirt will work. Graveyards are a whole 'nother thing. I am fortunate to live near enough to the burying places of many of my dead that I get to tend them. It is a privilege and it is also an obligation. In the African diaspora traditions, dirt from graveyards is used for many sorts of workings. I don't often take dirt from those sacred places unless I'm adding a bit of grounding to an Ancestor altar. Otherwise, I tend their resting places and find other kinds of dust for what I do.

Brick dust is a borry—mountain folks don't tend to use its protective properties. I run a line of it as a protective shielding at entryways and make small talismans for clients to give them an extra sense of protection, especially if they are feeling vulnerable in some ways. I no longer use brick dust, per se—I grind up red clay from our legendary red clay soil and use that.

Epsom salts—mercy, this stuff is good for all kinds of things. I use magnesium sulfate for compounds for workings involving calming and relaxation.

Salt—I keep at least three grades of salt at all times. A box of fine-grained table salt, big kosher salt and something beautiful like a fleur de sel. It is useful for a variety of workings and is one of the best filtration systems known.

Baking soda—sodium bicarbonate is as useful as Epsom salts. Cheap, readily available. It is a sovereign cleaning product, and that's how I use it. I fill small jars, sachets and the like with it to clean up ugly or toxic situations.

Ground coffee—give it to honor your land spirits (or to wake them up). Mix it with refined sugar and sprinkle as an offering.

String and Twine. The little packets of spellwork that are called sachets are usually tied together with available twine. The tough narrow cord that is used on hay bales is called, oddly enough, baling twine. Sisal rope from the garden center is also good for tying and for bindings. Embroidery thread (or floss) is used for wrapping small and delicate workings, and fat acrylic knitting yarn is very good for use in egg bindings. I keep a ball of black and another of red for just those purposes.

Reflective surfaces

These are magical tools, used for divination and energetic repulsion. I generally speak of "reflective surfaces," rather than mirrors because I am as likely to recommend an aluminum pie pan as I am a pricey hand mirror. The Energy Trap in Chapter Six features the bottom of a disposable pie pan, for instance. My favorite reflective surface is also a mainstay of wild childhoods in the southern Highlands—mica, from micare—to glitter. I have a big block of it and pull off fine layers, using my thumbnail as a tool. It is easily obtained, can be used in sachets and other workings, and is wonderful in warding and shielding work. Commercially, mica is used as an insulator.

And pools of still water—from the cat's water bowl to the cooling water in a springhouse—are good places to scry and to interact with the spirits of place that abound in the southern Highlands.

Staubs, Steel, and Iron

Have you been wondering now—for all these pages—what a "staub" is? This is a good place to talk about it, and I thought I'd begin by finding out where the word comes from. I did an Internet search and couldn't find it anywhere. Because I was spelling it the way it sounds when people around here say it— staub—and not the way it is actually spelled—stob. You know how stubborn we mountain folks are—I kept my original spelling.

"Stob" comes from Middle English, as a variant of "stub." It means a short, stout piece of wood, often driven into the ground. In my experience, it is bigger than a standard stake but not as big as a post. (The American Heritage® Dictionary of the English Language, Fourth Edition.)

Staubs are set for a variety of reasons. They are sometimes set as a marker on a property line. They can be set as a warning. Staubs are sometimes used in placing permanent or semipermanent wards around a piece of land. Ancestors can be honored with a staub, beneath which you can set little offerings and remembrances.

The most dramatic use of a staub is to set your intention. You can write that intention directly on the staub, anoint it with oil or an appropriate water, and then have the pleasure of hammering it into the ground, to make it stick.

A staub can be made from any kind of wood, but a hardwood is best. I suspect many a mountain woman used a piece of kindling in the old days of wood stoves, and that would be effective too.

All these years after the Iron Age, metal is still precious. There are some things that can't be wrought with wood or stone, and the sharp edge of metal tools can work in subtle ways. Many modern Pagan folks have ceremonial knives and swords, and those are used as conductors of personal energy—and often as pretty accessories for ritual wear.

I keep several knives handy most of the time. Two belonged to my own grandmother—one is an Old Hickory and the other is a nameless blade that is so worn there's a curve in it. Knives are used for slicing, cutting, chopping... you know what knives are for. I use them for herbs and other materials that need to be chopped.

I loved those old hardware stores where there were barrels and spinning metal display units of nails. You bought nails by the pound then, getting as few or as many as you needed for a given project. Nails come in a dizzying array of sizes and kinds, and I encourage you to go to a local hardware store, if you have one, and spend half an hour amongst the nails. I have a particular fondness for barbed-wire staples—those fat, dull, U-shaped nails that are hard to drive but so effective.

Horseshoes that have been cast and are no longer useable have a long history as keepers of luck and goodness. A horseshoe over the doorway brings luck to the house, but it must always be hung points up, to keep the luck from running out.

A Mercury/silver dime is believed to be effective in curing a number of ills, chief among them related to teeth, tooth pain, and teething. A silver dime with a hole in it was often worn around the neck of teething children to help the teeth come in straight and strong.

This is one of my favorite "metals," and I love to use them for money-drawing workings—chocolate coins. They are generally available in December, and I try to stock up on them for use throughout the year. I have to wonder though—is this a borry from the Jewish tradition?

Much of folk magic is about using tools you love and are familiar to you. People who do some actual writing with an instrument on paper will have a favorite style of pen or pencil that they prefer. I like those Black Warrior pencils and pick up a pack during the back-to-school sales in the late summer. I also have my grandmother's carpenter pencil—the kind that's flat so it won't roll away. Those peel-away grease pencils can be handy too. I've never lost my love of crayons and use them sometimes to lay in a batch of bright color for a working.

PAPER

There's an old truism about where the Sears and Roebuck catalogue (the Wish Book) ended up in the days when you went to the bathroom in a small building with a crescent moon on its door. But mountain people always have had a knack for making do, using available materials, recycling. Many people use fabric for pocket sachets, but the traditional material was found paper, like those good old catalogues. Later on, brown paper was used, and it's good to have a supply of that on your workbench.

EGGS

Eggs may be the universal material for binding, for fertility work, for holding secrets in their rich yellow hearts. I did a working several years ago for a Brazilian woman who was visiting her brother here. She spoke little English, and we worked with a translator, which was interesting. My client seemed a little dubious of getting the kind of help from me that she would get from someone in her own tradition, and the language barrier didn't help. But when I opened the cloth on my work-basket and pulled out some eggs, a grease pencil, and some red embroidery floss, she visibly relaxed. She told the translator that she finally had some faith in me when she saw the eggs and the red thread.

Essay Three

Baba Yaga in the Sacred Landscape

My email inbox is the frequent recipient of outraged and sorrowing emails about the state of Stonehenge in England and the Hill of Tara in Ireland. Both places have been important cultural markers in my personal spiritual journey, and I have been awed and privileged to spend time at each monument. Both are endangered, say the emails, by the coming of new development. A new road is being cut through the valley near Tara, and the historically important plains around The Great Henge will soon host a giant Tesco warehouse. It feels to many people as though it is a desecration of the sacred landscape that is vital to the cultural identity of those two places and to the spiritual identity of modern Pagans all over the world.

I've been thinking about the landscape lately—how could I not? Every time I turn around, someone is stripping the trees off a section of fragile hillside and planting a cluster of goofy-looking structures on it. As much as I love Tara and Wiltshire, my sacred landscape is here in the mountains that hold my Ancestors' bones and ashes. I've watched the changes of the past decades, and some of them fit the pattern of change in Asheville: Pack Square gets transformed periodically, and I feel sure every generation that witnesses and pays for the change gripes and grumbles. There were "White Only" bathrooms underground in Pack Square in the 1970s—losing those was a vast improvement. But the IM Pei Building? The BB&T Building? That is a matter of opinion, of taste, of history in the landscape.

The last time I was in his chair, my periodontist started a discussion about the proposed Ellington. Isn't that always the way? There's a couple of hands and sharp instruments in my mouth, and the nurse occasionally inserts a little vacuum hose, but we somehow manage not only to have an in-depth conversation about the felling of the Enka smokestacks but to sing that song about using a baseball bat on your cheating man's truck.

Like myself, the good doctor is a native of this place, and we started reminiscing about the things that we miss: the Imperial Theatre, the old Coleman House, Valkyrie Farms in Enka, the Back Alley Boutique. It's what natives do around here. A few days later, I met with a local author out on Smoky Park Highway. I had a good view of the former Enka plant because I was sitting in a coffee shop where the Valkyrie Farm used to be. We talked about downtown Enka, with its drugstore and gas station. All gone now, the stuff of anecdote.

Natives talk about how our granddads went to the Man Store or about the Goat Man who lived in Emma. We're insufferable that way—what must the newcomers think, those people who have no roots and don't care to have any? My roots make my head spin sometimes, make my back ache with the loss and the turmoil. The Ellington is the least of my worries. There are whole blocks and opera houses and neighborhoods that have been lost in this place.

Lately, I've taken to blaming it all on the Baba Yaga. Baba Yaga comes out of the Russian folk tradition, and she flies through the air in a mortar, using the pestle as a rudder. In fairy tales, she is a Hag who is mostly avoided but occasionally sought out for her expert advice. She is opinionated and inscrutable, as all older women are, and she can't be relied upon to behave as she should. Just ask the Obama campaign about independent older women, and that goes double for the Baba Yaga.

It is somewhat bad form for one witch to blame another, but I've noticed that her houses have sprung up on the west bank of the French Broad River, and that is a sure sign she is in residence. There's a line of them, silhouetted against the evening sky, and they strike terror into the heart of anyone who sees them. They are perched on chicken legs, high on the bank. Houses that defy gravity, the wind whistling around their steel supports—how do you insulate such a place?

Who lives in a Baba Yaga house on chicken legs and how much have they paid? How much do we pay for the systematic destruction of our sacred landscape? When we lose that ineffable spirit, we can't regain it or return to it. It will take more than the Baba Yaga to bring back the feeling of home and place that is easy to sense but hard to define.

As we creep forward into this time of inflation and recession and campaign ads, I wonder if the economy will slow the development and destruction of my personal sacred landscape. I resolve to take it up with that Wise Woman of the Woods, the Baba Yaga, and to remember that one only approaches her if the need is great. The approach must be carefully planned, one's intention pure and it's always good to practice unfailing good manners.

Just like you'd approach your grandma.

CHAPTER FOUR

STANDING ON THE KNOLL: DIVINATION AND OMEN-READING

In my mind's eye, I am Maria Ouspenskaya as Maleva the Gypsy Woman in the original *Wolf Man* movie. Or I am Toady and Rat, setting out on an adventure on the open road in Kenneth Grahame's *The Wind in the Willows*. There are grainy photos of me aged about five, with a scarf on my head, scrying my grandmother's heavy water globe, sitting by the piano bench.

There is no Roma blood in my family, and I live in the same neighborhood my great-grandmother settled in at the end of the nineteenth century. What is it about being a "gypsy" woman that follows me, makes me dream of hand-painted round wagons, pulled by stout ponies?

I reckon it's all about reading the future.

History and literature are full of shady characters who claim to see the future. Shakespeare had them, Hollywood films feature them, but all this begs the question—why would anyone really want to know the future? It seems like something handy, but if you stop and think through it, would you want to know what's going to happen to you?

Would it help to mitigate a dire circumstance or give you the heads-up on a memory you want to absorb every last drop of?

Perhaps. But I suspect we want to know what's going to happen for reasons having more to do with curiosity than preparation. Some clients want to know if their gut feeling about a particular future event is justified, and sometime they merely want to get a rough idea of what to expect.

If we spend ten minutes either reading or listening to the news, it's full of predictions about the future. The stock market has a segment that deals in futures. Pundits are always speculating about what this event or that will lead to. Heaven knows anything to do with the economy seems to have more to do with guesswork than skill or knowledge. I suspect the ability to sacrifice a chicken and read its entrails is as valuable as knowing economic theory. And you could at least have a delicious meal afterward.

Looking into the distance—either the future or the distance between two people—is practiced through numerous divinatory practices and in the reading of signs and omens. The old folks did it for all sorts of reasons, and the savvy modern rootworker, urban homesteader, and organic gardener would be wise to learn the old techniques and to create new ones. I'm often surprised when Witches and Pagans of my acquaintance don't practice these simple and homely arts.

I indulge in it all the time, whether invited to or not. Facebook allows for many chances to think through an occurrence that is puzzling to friends. We humans love to make meaning even where there is none, but sometimes the explanations are clear as spring water.

A pastor colleague posted that he'd stepped out of the rented mountain cabin where he and his wife were vacationing and a snake fell off the roof onto the path. What did that mean, he wondered. I started peppering him with questions—what kind of snake was it? Did it fall in front of you or behind you? Which way did it go, assuming it skittered off?

From Caesar to the Psychic hotline to the "Gypsy fortuneteller" at the Fall Fair, the variety of people who read the signs is diverse and interesting. I personally believe that all those TV talking heads that predict what the economy is going to do in the next months ought to be replaced with a decent card reader. Same thing really—information, intuition, and experience come together in the person of the prognosticator, and there is some hope that the information is accurate.

We're going to start with some simple definitions and travel out from there. These words are often used interchangeably by the uninitiated, but they involve different techniques and sometimes different tools. Here's our knotty list for looking forward and backward through what we think of as time: sign, omen, intuition, divination, and premonition.

A sign is something natural and observed. You plant corn when the oak leaf is the size of a squirrel's ear. The waning moon is the best time to plant below-ground crops.

An omen is something natural, observed, and unusual. The snake that rolled off that cabin roof at that time was natural and observed but also unusual. Crows flying in an unfamiliar pattern are often omens.

Let's compare the two things—a young deer racing across the interstate might be a sign if it is frequently observed in your area but may be considered an omen if it is unusual. (We'll speak a little more about this farther along.) A yard full of robins in January means more snow. A yard full of robins in May means you don't have outdoor cats.

Intuition is what you know in the pit of your stomach. When we say, "trust your gut," we are inviting you to listen to that small voice of your inner wisdom, your intuition. "I've got a bad feeling about this" is often the phrase that comes a few hours before you say, "I should've listened to my gut."

Divination is the act (and the art) of purposefully looking into the future to see what's going to happen next. There are lots of interesting and fun tools for this, and there are techniques for divination that require no tools at all.

A premonition is a sign or omen that usually indicates something dire and dangerous. Though the word can be used to mean any precognitive information, in the mountains it is almost always used to presage something bad.

All of these require the participant to be observant and to know the place that is your place. A couple of years ago, a friend asked me to come to her house at dusk and observe the weird things the crows were doing. We sat on her back stoop and talked quietly as the shadows lengthened. At last a family group of crows came in silently to nest in the tall trees at the back of her yard. They complained and grumbled until everyone got in their place and my friend said—"now, wait." Within a minute or so, one member of the almost-settled family began cawing a loud, insistent note. There was a pause, and then that sharp cry was heard again. My friend looked at me quizzically.

"What does that mean? Isn't that weird? It makes me very nervous."

"Wait," I said. And we did. In a moment, a lone crow flew silently over our heads and into the nesting trees. A little more grumbling and then all was quiet.

You see, they'd gotten settled into a good nesting place and realized they weren't all there. So they set up a call to let the errant runabout know where they were. It didn't take long for that crow to find the others, and then all was well.

It didn't seem scary or weird to me because I observe crows and know some of their behaviors. But it seemed ominous to my friend because of the cultural overtones related to crows as well as the noise that felt threatening. When she understood what was really going on, the whole thing lost its mystery and became another thing that wild birds do.

A conversation with an online friend brought up this interchange about the nature of the individual bird-bringers and what that would all mean. She had seen a wren, a mockingbird, and an owl—all behaving unusually and all near her.

In my work, birds are always messengers from the Divines, and we are wise to observe them and look for additional meaning. I interpreted my friend's omen to mean that change had happened and it wasn't over yet. She had three very interesting bringers: a wee songbird, a trickster, and the Western symbol of silent wisdom. It can be as simple as—you are wise to find the joy in the midst of change and will be rewarded if you continue to do the same. But always watch that little trickster—mockingbirds help dispel illusion, if we will only heed their appearance and keep our eyes open. Besides, they are fun to watch.

If you are going to take up reading signs, it is vitally important that you know what's what in the natural world around you. What happens in the morning when the sun rises? When does winter usually come? What are the signs of earliest spring, and what are the signs of true spring?

These require you to be situated in a place for several seasons, so if you are a natural wanderer, it will be a little trickier for you to discern what is natural and normal versus what is unusual in your microclimate.

Omen-reading is an individual practice, and you can learn much by talking to other diviners in your area. Your personal observations can be jotted down and checked as a reference against what happens later. You can "check the math" on an omen by remembering that time you saw a ring around the moon and a weather change came twenty-four hours later. Observe that again and see if it holds true.

There is a difference between omen-reading and divination, though both are very useful and informative. Omen-reading is reading what comes to you from your omen-bringers. Divination is seeking out the answers through tools and techniques that bring you specifics about an event or occurrence. The two can complement each other, of course. You may observe an omen and then get out the cards or other tools for clarification and more information.

In addition to these, it is common to "ask" for a sign when you are unsure of a decision or desired outcome. Should I take this job? After weighing the practical pros and cons of the offer, you may choose to ask your guides or spirit animals, your saints or gods for a sign. As you develop your skills, you will find that specific beings and animals will act as omen-bringers for you. Mountain folks sometimes ask Luke for a sign (though they don't think of him as Saint Luke) because he wrote the most familiar nativity story and must have been a good observer. It is also common to ask a deceased relative for guidance by way of a sign, especially when in doubt about a proposal of marriage.

Who are some of the other omen-bringers you might encounter as you are learning this craft? As mentioned earlier, birds are often considered reliable omen-bringers, and this is true cross-culturally. One could argue that birds are everywhere, are easily observed and their high level of mobility as well as their size gives them an advantage as omen-bringers.

What birds are common in your area? Not only your yard but the place you work, the highways and byways of your particular microclimate—all of these offer opportunities to "read" your avian neighbors. When traveling by car, it's easy to observe the birds that fly across your path, as well as the raptors that may be riding the thermals above the roadway. I've developed a simple and effective quick read of crows— one that I employ whenever I'm out and about.

If a crow flies from right to left in front of me, it means "No worries. All is well. Conditions favorable."

If a crow flies from left to right, it means "Watch your back. Energies shifting. Take care."

A crow flying from the front to the back of the car (and away into the place I've just been) indicates that the answer to questions and concerns lies in a deep study of the past, either my personal past or the historic past. Have I dealt with the situation before? What did I do and what was the outcome?

A crow flying from behind me to disappear ahead of me indicates that it is time to dream, to vision into the future, to find an answer in the dreamtime or through trance work.

All this may be very different for you. Remember this kind of omen-reading is personal and specific. You begin by observing the critters in your neighborhood. Who lives near you? Are they there throughout the year or do they migrate or hibernate? Our annual and national obsession with groundhogs is all about weather prognostication, raised to the level of a jolly holiday. But those critters go to ground every winter, so using a groundhog as an omen-bringer means you'll need to switch to something else in the coldest seasons.

The most reliable thing to do is to develop a relationship with several different omen-bringers and styles of omen-reading. Maybe you live in the woods and you read bear scat throughout the late spring and summer. When the bears go to ground for the winter, you may choose to read other signs or to have an alternate omen-bringer. Here in North Carolina, the cardinal is the state bird, and he is often chosen for his brightness during the long gray months between the high-color season and the earliest spring.

Our Ancestors, as well as modern gardeners and farmers, relied on reading signs to do planting, harvesting, butchering and other homely and important acts. There are elaborate signs for planting here in the southern Highlands. The weather is unpredictable, especially in the spring. Corn isn't planted until the oak leaf is the size of a squirrel's ear—which means you must observe both leaf and ear. Potatoes are planted after the first full moon following St. Patrick's Day. And you never set out tomato plants until after Easter (though I often wait if Easter is early).

Above-ground plants go into the ground in the light of the moon, which means a waxing moon. Root crops go in during the dark of the moon—a waning moon. When I was little, I thought people went out by moonlight (or lack thereof) to plant parts of the garden. Planting in the light of the moon seemed easy, but I wondered how you planted when there wasn't any moonlight. I soon learned that the planting part happens during regular daylight hours and the observing of the moon phase is the part that happens at night. Or during the day, reading your favorite farmers' almanac.

Harvesting hay and corn or cutting shingles for the roof are all governed by the sign of the moon—and the weather. At a local state historic site that consists of acres of fields and original buildings from the early nineteenth century, we were rewarded with a story of just how important this sign reading still is in some quarters.

Our guide that day was an older man—and someone from around here—who drew our attention to the new wooden shingles on one of the outbuildings. He'd had it on his to-do list and was waiting for the right sign. But he went on vacation and one of his coworkers decided to get that little job done. He didn't cut the shingles in the right moon sign, thinking that was some old superstition that didn't matter in the modern world. He went ahead and cut the shingles and shingled the roof.

When the older man got back from vacation, he was surprised to see the work done but kept his mouth shut about the results. The younger fellow who'd roofed the building was proud of the straight rows and matching shingles, and laughed at the notion that you had to wait for the moon. The roof looked great!

You know the end of this story. All those shingles curled up and the whole thing had to be redone—new shingles cut and cured (during the right sign), old shingles removed and the new roof installed.

Many days of work that could have been avoided—simply by paying attention to the signs and knowing the value of those old mountain "superstitions."

DIVINATORY TOOLS AND TECHNIQUES

As we discussed before, intuition is what you know in the pit of your stomach. Divination is the act and art of looking into the future to see what's going to happen next.

It is handy to have a divination technique and tool at your beck and call. If you don't have one already, cards are a good place to start. They are easily transportable, can be read most anywhere, are easy to replace if they become lost or stolen. Though anyone who would steal a deck of tarot cards may be asking for more than they bargained for.

I learned to read regular playing cards when I was about twelve and upped my game a few years later with an Aquarian Tarot deck's Major Arcana that came from a Scholastic book fair. When I finally got my hands on a whole entire Smith-Rider-Waite deck, I never looked back. Clients and new friends shake their heads in wonder when I tell them I've been reading cards for more than forty years.

When I work with students, we always begin with a simple and timeless tool—the cootie catcher. Most of us made those when we were kids—an origami tool of colors and numbers that will tell you if someone likes you or if you're going to do well on a test.

There are many other divination tools, and many of them are culturally based. From runes, bones, and scrying balls to shells, stones and animal guts, divinatory tools are as varied and diverse as the people who use them.

In addition to observing nature, learning how to shuffle a very large deck of cards, and mastering the art of unfocusing your eyes to scry some ditchwater, you'd be wise to spend some time in studying common symbols and what they mean. For fun, let's choose thirteen symbols and attach meaning to them through practice and experimentation. Start with these—dog, flower, water, mountain, road, boat, person/doll, tree, egg, box, hat, sun, moon.

These are simple shapes that could appear in many kinds of readings, from tea leaves to dream interpretation to cloud scrying. You can use your intuition to reckon what each symbol could mean and do several trial-and-error tests to double-check your gut feeling. As you are cultivating your skills in reading signs and in divination, you will need to be scrupulous in checking your results. I can't emphasize enough what an individual practice this is. In the same way you decide what the direction of a pendulum means to you, you also will determine what these symbols mean for you, in your practice.

It's good to include a meaning and its opposite. In a case where the object being used for divination can reveal a symbol either upside down or reversed, it's helpful to think about the opposite of what each thing also means.

As an example, here are my personal interpretations of the symbols. The first is the positive interpretation. The reverse is within the parentheses.

Dog: loyalty (smothering attention)
Flower: affection (unrequited longing)
Water: gentle change (uncontrolled change)
Mountain: challenge (difficulty)
Road: travel (escape)
Boat: luxury (loss of resources)
Person/doll: influence (overbearing person)
Tree: growth (unyielding)
Egg: creativity (fear of success)
Box: safety (frustration)
Hat: status (pretension)
Sun: clarity (too many choices)
Moon: mystery (secrets kept)

There will also be situations in which you find two or more symbols in the same reading, so there are many combinations possible. Start with a few of them and see how it goes.

As I grow older, my uses of divination have grown more subtle. It is less about that tall, handsome stranger and more about working with the energy of the specific time. I've learned over the years that no matter how auspicious the time is, if the person for whom I'm divining hasn't the will to do what must be done or is so bogged down in loving their disease or situation, no good will come of it. It is one of the saddest and most frustrating parts of my practice and my work with clients. Oddly enough, there are people who are so wedded to their physical or psychic ailments that they won't budge from them, no matter what sort of receipt or working or reading comes their way.

You can try the One-Two-Three Brick wall method outlined in the following chapter, and it will give you an opportunity to try a variety of techniques. But you may never have any real success with those clients. They require a deep, interior and drastic move from where they are to the possibility of where they could be. If they have no hope in things ever changing or if they derive some sort of status from remaining where they are, your work will be in vain.

Caveat—whichever method of divination you choose, you will need to check the laws in your area. Yes, in this day and age, there are plenty of places where it is still illegal to practice "fortune-telling." So take time to check that out. Word to the wise.

ESSAY FOUR

My City Mother Has Risen From the Dead

I have thirsty roots in this place. Almost every day some fresh-faced newcomer whose grandma was born outland approaches me to learn where I'm from. Here, I say. When did you move here? I have always been here, like Pisgah and the Rat. Like the ghost woman who jumps for love of a dead man. I go away for a time and I always come back, for my gnarly roots seek refreshment from dark springs of mountain water. McKinney Cove. Enka High School. West End. You mean Chicken Hill? Hell, no. I mean West End. Bootleggers, murderers, so lawless that people from outside—people from Biltmore Forest, say—would threaten their wayward children with abandonment after nightfall in West End. In Peck Town. Mill workers and the concubines of rich men. Little children falling to an almost death through the rusty railings at Queen Carson School, only to be made to walk home, where they could die later. My grandfather coughing his way through TB on Jefferson, dying rough, the way "Sweet Stuff" had lived since he left the Navy, returning from the gassed fields of France. Rich in story and history, no doubt. A place of mythic stature. Steinbeck or Joyce or Williams got nothing to compare to it. Filth and squalor and soul-killing poverty. Ah, West End. Some flatland real estate developer from off can try to sell the Chicken Hill label, but it's an insult to the leveling of the real Chicken Hill, razed to story by the coming of the Expressway.

We don't have *Southern Living*-kind of Southerners in this family. We are more the "hell, no, we'll never forget" NASCAR kind of Southerners. We live in a landscape haunted by our personal demons and the familial boogers of our extended families. I always begin my life at Number Ten Roberts Street—the store and house where my great-grandmother raised ten children to maturity, or what counts as maturity in this family. A host of girls and three boys, all dead now. The oldest and the youngest, being for several years the only ones left, are both gone as I write this. If family can ever be gone. As if they cannot rise from Green Hill Cemetery and pace Park Square again, watching the clouds for winged angels.

I never saw Number Ten Roberts Street except in my mind's eye because my family left West End

in the last years of the Great Depression. Number
Ten holds the essence of Grandma and Grandpa
who came here from Haywood County, to escape in-
laws or bastard children or debt, who knows? I have
photographs of the wooden store, one with Grandma
in a filthy apron, standing with three boys in the
doorway, an advertisement near her shoulders. But
there is no photograph of upstairs at Number Ten and
no photograph of the couch where the ghost of the
dead man lay, on evenings when the streetlight shone
through the curtains. My mother saw him, as did my
grandmother as a young girl. He lay there with his
knees drawn up and his hand under his cheek, sweet
and peaceful and long dead. No one knew him—he
was not one of ours. But he inhabited the upstairs at
Number Ten on those nights, a temporary permanent
visitor. He was there since before the flood of 1916
and may have been there when they tore the structure
down during the halcyon days of Urban Renewal.
Plans are drawn to put an artist's studio on the square
of land and I wonder sometimes if the sleeping man
will appear on some paint-spattered sofa in the loft,
relieved to find a napping place.

People genuinely from here can blink their eyes
and see Pack Square in its reincarnations, have a heart
for the old Wall Street, bought feed and seed in T.
S. Morrison's. We can remember heavy traffic on
Tunnel Road as lines of reeking cars popped through
the old tunnel, before the Cut was cut. In West End,
you can blink your eyes and the street cars are running
again, a bulky school building dominates the hilltop,
the river rises into Miss Olive's basement, and Ida

Crawley floats below the captain's walk on her turret, frightening the children.

But I digress, wandering again through the stories and places that made me and made my family, denizens at Number Ten who climbed out of West End and the mill. My grandmother's stories became my stories, my mother's stories became mine, my elder-cousins bequeathed me variations on a theme of this peopled empty space. A great-aunt put a board out the upstairs window onto another balcony and escaped the baleful eye of her father, eloping with the boy she loved who would become a tyrant and a pervert. She would stay with him until he died, a relief (it was said) to anyone who had to submit to his constant lust.

Tyranny is a kind of theme to this place: the tyranny of the mill, the church, the parent, the spouse, the city government who forgot this oldest of neighborhoods and only remembered when it was time to excise something from it. Some land or some taxes or some drink during the years of Prohibition when a drink of liquor could always be found in West End. Batwing bottles of corn from Tennessee, hidden under rotting floor boards and in baby's bassinets. Satisfying ways for lazy men to make a buck while their women took in laundry or sewing or warmed eggs in their aprons to facilitate the birthing of chicks. Sometimes the men took mean and hit their women-wives-sisters or slammed the door on the tails of their cats. The men could be mean drunks, it is told, and so could the women. Once, a man so mean or sad or eviscerated with life shot his wife through the chest, the bullet going in here and coming out there. She appeared later in the clouds and my mother was whipped when she mentioned her, because looking up to heaven and seeing a neighbor there was somehow more shameful than shooting your wife.

Around the corner from Number Ten and slightly up the hill is Mary's House, one residence upstairs and an apartment in the basement, a not uncommon sight in West End. I never knew Mary's last name and can't remember who told me her first because I never spoke to her, not once. I sometimes sat with Mr. Guthrie and his white dogs but Mary never came out to her yard. She peeked out the window or stood at the door waiting. I saw her months after she died, still waving from the window, still waiting. Mr. Guthrie has gone from his old home place, visiting with my elders in the steeps of Green Hill. Sometimes I spot a whisk of white from the oldest ghost dog, trotting to the back of the restored and soulless old house.

My mother was born here, in a house that her mother did not own. Upstairs, across the street but still on the myth-full Roberts Street. She left when her mother did, but all my life she carried the joy of growing up poor in West End, where she and her friends smoked cigarettes at twelve and pretended they lived on a ranch in Texas. She met my father hereabouts and told of her grandmothers here, one for her mother and one for her father. I carry those tales now, Jacob Marley-style, never sure what is real and what is not. Not that truth matters in myth. After the war, she was moved to the western part of the county to a place she always hated, hated till the day she died, alone in the night with no one to hear her last confession if she spoke it.

When my mother died in a pre-9/11 world, we had worked nothing out between us. We had come to a Middle Eastern peace that was as unworkable as it was uneasy. We lived in this state of ungrace—too much unsaid, too much misunderstood, a wall of pain and anger towered between us—and so she died. My life is quieter for her absence from it, my parenting loving and conscious as it can be (given what it is), a legacy of her laissez-faire approach to affection, her bitter-honed edge of rebuke and complaint always present. I count myself lucky to no longer receive the late-night drunken calls that invite me to shatter the portable phone against the front of the piano in my fury. She did not haunt me until now, preferring to give me a false sense of security, to think I had at last escaped. She has risen, I must tell you, from the dead. I saw her only a few days ago in my sister's house, inhabiting my sister's body, looking at me through my sister's eyes.

What to do now? She cannot be vanquished, a lesson I learned in my adulthood. No matter how I plot, she can turn my good intent to malice, my best work as dust before her glance. She will join those others who walk the narrow ruts of West End streets, waiting for another turn at a life hard in its living. Only Mrs. Crawley is above this fray of spirits, pacing her porch roof, shaking her sad head.

CHAPTER FIVE

A PECK OF HELPFUL RECEIPTS: TRADITIONAL OR OF MY OWN DEVISING

In the first chapter, I referenced the old metal recipe box from a mythical great-aunt's kitchen. Here at the end of the book are some additions for your own recipe box. These are some workings, charms, and banes that I use in my practice. It's a sampling of what can be done, with materials and instructions. Write them out and tuck them in your file, scribbling your changes and additions in the margins, griming it up with your wet thumbprints and a little red clay mud.

GROUNDING

Sit comfortably with your feet flat on the floor and your hands loose in your lap. Begin breathing, deep belly breaths. Wiggle your toes and press your feet into the floor, really feeling the connection. Drop that connection through the layers of flooring (assuming you're inside) until you feel the earth beneath.

(I always liken this to hugging someone in a winter coat. Just because you are both wearing down jackets, it doesn't mean you can't hug another person. Same with earth—there may be a layer of concrete and rug and wood and whatever between you and actual soil, but those are only coverings.)

Imagine the coolness of it and the damp. Feel tiny roots grow from the bottoms of your feet down into the soil. As they stretch and grow, they become fatter and stronger, until they reach deep into the crust of the earth.

Breathe, breathe.

Now imagine that your feet are empty, nothing inside. Feel this openness travel up your calves and knees, through your thighs and hips and bottom, all the way to your belly button. Let it rest there.

Now let the energy level rise up through those open spaces and fill the lower half of your body with strong, supporting, green earth energy.

Breathe, breathe.

Shake your hands out and roll your shoulders a bit to loosen up your upper body. Open your mouth wide and yawn. Make a sound. Connect the upper part of your body to the lower, and when you feel that connection, put your hand flat against your belly button.

Wiggle your feet again, imagining that your roots are moveable and that you take this rooted connection with you wherever you go. Stand and stretch upward, as though you are picking apples from a tall tree. Breathe deeply into your whole body.

Personal shielding should be high on your list of skills.

Ground yourself and breathe deeply. Imagine this: in front of you raise a curved wall of clear green Emerald, higher than your head. At your right hand, raise up a similar curved wall of Diamond. At your back, the protective wall is transparent Ruby. On your left hand, raise up a curved wall of clear blue Sapphire. Let each of these walls connect at the edges with the next one so that you are encased in an impenetrable wall that is clear enough to gaze through. Nothing comes in, nothing goes out. Breathe and allow yourself the gift of relaxing fully, of taking in no information from any source—material or noncorporeal. It is a place to regroup, to get your bearings, a lull in the energy storm of your day-to-day life. Use this when you need respite.

Ideally, you can do all of this swiftly. Three snaps of the fingers—ground, center, shield. Regroup, strategize, emerge.

How To Construct and Use an Energy Trap

This is one of the most helpful things ever—a HEPA filter for all the yucky energy in your home, office, or car.

Here's what you need to gather up:

a flat, round reflective surface (the bottom of a throwaway pie pan is the best, but you can use a round mirror too)

three flat black rocks
The Jewel Case
a tea-light candle (My preference is battery-operated because they are safe around children and animals. Definitely use that if you do one of these for your car.)
two grades of salt

I use inexpensive table salt and kosher salt. Place the reflective surface on a flat surface—put it on a high shelf out of sight, if that's needed or put it in a prominent place to add the energy of your thoughts every time you see it. Put the three flat stones in the center of the mirror. Pour the kosher salt in a circle around the stones. Pour the table salt on the outer edge of the mirror. Place the tea light on top of the stones in the center and light it or turn it on. The theory—stagnant and unhealthy energy is drawn to the light, filtered first through the stones, then filtered through the rough salt, then filtered a final time through the fine salt. It is then reflected back out into the area as clean, useable energy. You can keep one of these going all the time, but it isn't necessary. You'll feel the difference in a few days. If you are moving into a new place or if your office environment is harsh, run the trap for at least a moon cycle. If you run it longer than that, change the salt every moon cycle. ONE-TWO-THREE... BRICK WALL! What if it doesn't work? A rule of thumb I have for workings is this: my first pass-through takes into consideration the seriousness of the job, and I apply what I believe to be an appropriate amount of effort and energy for it. If it doesn't achieve the desired results—either through a lack of complete information or my own slackass attitude—I rethink, regroup and restructure and take another run at it. If that doesn't work, then I gather all resources (astrology, moon cycle, season, ancestors, etc.), and I give it one more enormous push. If it doesn't work that time—brick wall—I know it isn't for me to do at this time and I put down my toolbox and bow to a greater will.

On a similar note—I met a writer and energy worker who has created a system of "strategic sorcery." As he describes it, I think of it as the Howitzer Method. Basically, he sets up a hierarchically tiered working that begins with the "lower powers" and is literally built like a tower on his altar. I'm studying his methods now and will add it to our arsenal as I find it useful.

However you determine to enter into the work, consider all these options and allies when doing a job of work—land spirits and noncorporeal allies ("power animals"), ancestors, earth energies, celestial energies, personal energy, personal will, tools and materials, other energy-workers, your teachers/teachers and your personal deities.

Busting a Glamour: Seeing What's What

If someone is trying to pull the wool over your eyes, it's time to get out from under the covers.

Nothing to gather up for this one—except your nerve. A glamour is a personal spell for personal advancement of some kind. Often you will encounter a glamour in meetings where it's important to one of the participants to get the attention of (or the upper-hand on) everyone else in the room. With experience, you can sometimes smell a glamour—I'm not kidding. But if you are sitting in a group (or alone with another person) and you can't figure out why that person is getting such a sweet reception from the gathered folks, there may be a glamour at work. If you are sitting with another person and can't figure out why you are hanging on their every work, that's a glamour.

It is a very old technique, very useful, and often done in the most unconscious of ways. Some of them are innocent enough—when you go to court, you want the judge to see you as the injured party or as a competent witness or whatnot. But often the point of the glamour is to get ahead of people who have worked harder or are more knowledgeable than the glamour-caster. And glamours are easy to bust.

Ground yourself and start listening and smelling. Start deep breathing to clear your energy field. When you are ready to start, simply sit with your forearms resting on your thighs. Open up your left hand, palm up, and begin tapping the center of that palm with the middle finger of your right hand. You'll start to feel the one hand get warm and then the other. When the energy feels to be flowing back and forth between the tapping hand and the receiving hand, look up at the person you believe is "glamoured." No need to glare or give them the stink-eye—simply let your eyes rest upon them and keep tapping. Soon you will be rewarded with seeing the person as they really are—tired, shaky, afraid, nervous. Give a little nod of thanks and keep tapping, if you want to expose the glamour to the other people assembled. Listen and feel the shifting of energies in the room. You may be rewarded with seeing the whole crazy house of cards come tumbling down.

GOOD HEALTH

First thing anybody ought to tell you is—get some sleep, take a walk, drink water. But there's also a little more you can do in the do-feel-good department.

There are lots of remedies from the southern Highlands, but that's not our purpose here. We want to gather up some good healing energy and pour it all over us or help a client whose interest is regaining or strengthening their health. Here's what you need to gather up:

dried chamomile
dirt from your land
dried mugwort
dried lavender
dried rosemary
uncooked rice/grain/corn dried hops

Make a little pillow, about the size of a 3x5-inch index card. Use enough of the dried herbs to stuff it full, adding pinches of the dirt and grain. The theory— you are remembering good health. The grain will absorb the dis-ease, the dirt will ground the client (or you) and the herbs will stimulate the dream-self to embrace robust physical health.

Good Luck

Don't forget—our natural state is lucky. First off, sweep from the front door of your house to the back, leaving both doors open. Ah, let the energy and sweet cold air flow through.

Here's what you need to gather up—a little bit of your own dirt (even from a flower pot), some dried vervain, chamomile, and a whole nutmeg if you've got one. Ground nutmeg will do in a pinch. Get yourself a plain brown bag and cut a square shape out of it—about 4x4 inches. Get yourself some red string, like embroidery floss. Put all your dry ingredients in the middle of the square and stir them around with the pointer finger of your nondominant hand. Find a little shiny something—piece of glass or mirror, beads, you know—shiny. Put that in the middle of your dirt-n-herbs. Take that same finger and tap the top three times, thinking to yourself how lucky you are going to be this year. Now fold that paper over on itself tight so nothing falls out. Tie it up tight with the red string, into a small package. Tap it one more time, same as before, thinking the same things. Place that little sachet to your forehead, to your eyes, to your mouth, to your belly and finally over your heart. Keep it with you as you can—in purse or wallet or pocket. Take it out every full moon and let it recharge, always reminding yourself—my natural state is lucky, very lucky.

Receipt for Rue Oil

Sometimes it's just too hard to find an Amazing Rue candle.

Pack a pint Mason jar with fresh cuttings from a rue plant. Include leaves, flowers and stems, if possible. Fill the jar with vegetable oil and allow it to steep for a moon cycle. Decant the oil and remove any extra rue bits because the fresh herb will mold. I add some amber stones to the oil.

Prosperity: The Happy Pocketbook

Don't be thinking of money as a bad thing or of yourself as a bad person for wanting some.

Here's what you need to gather up:

a little coin purse (the best are those old-fashioned ones with a little clasp on top) that can open into a wide "mouth"
shiny coins of any denomination (even chocolate ones will work)
a small mirror
green candle/s
a pinch of instant coffee or a few coffee beans
individually wrapped hard candies

This is such a fun working—I keep one going all the time. And it's easy. I have mine on my altar, but you can put it anywhere that you'll see it and add energy to it. Set your little coin purse upright with its mouth open. Plunk in some shiny coins and set all manner of shiny things around it. Set up the mirror so that it reflects the purse. Put the green candle (I always use a glass jar or seven-day candle) near and burn it as much as possible. You can also use those battery-operated tea lights and leave it going all the time. Keep a lookout for shiny coins coming to you as change and add them to the purse. Any "found" coins also go in and around the purse. Periodically add a pinch of instant coffee to the coins and purse to keep gathering energy. And don't forget to leave some bright candies for your house and land spirits and ask them to welcome all your abundance/prosperity/money energy. Enjoy!

An Altar for Attracting a Job

(with thanks to Sabra)

Let the right job see me!

My friend Sabra had graduated from school and was a little anxious about getting a good job—one that suited her and would give her the kind of money to start repaying those student loans. I suggested creating an attraction altar. As big or small as she liked and including some white candles—so the right job would see her. I proposed a combination of battery tea lights and seven-day/jar candles and that she anoint them with whatever come-hither seemed to work best for her. At the center of the altar, I suggested she put a clear bowl of willow water (water that has had willow stems soaking in it, plus some willow leaves in the water). Then sprinkle the whole thing with Irish moss and Spanish moss so that the right job not only saw her but that the attention sticks. I might even toss some cockleburs on the altar, too, for stick-ability.

LOVE (OKAY, REALLY LUST)

It is never a good idea to do a specific love spell because they always work and it's always a nightmare. Lust, however, is a whole 'nother thing.

Here's what you need to gather up: rose water, cotton balls (hey, watch that dirty mind!), chocolate to eat (pick your favorite), flower petals from any fragrant flower, a cinnamon stick, a medium-sized red apple.

Core the apple, remove the stem and eat the core, including the seeds. Soak the cotton balls in rose water and roll them in the flower petals. Stuff the center of the apple with the cotton balls and then push the cinnamon stick in too. (If your preference is non-penetrative nookie, leave out the cinnamon stick.) Lay the apple on its side and place your left hand palm down on the apple while you slowly eat the chocolate and think of the object of your lust. Bury the apple near flowing water and eat a bite of chocolate every day for seven days. On the seventh day, eat a teaspoon of raw, local honey.

RECEIPT FOR AN EGG BINDING

Eggs—they're not just for potato salad.

A binding is an energetic working in which the practitioner prevents a miscreant from harming other people through their actions. Take a fresh raw egg. Write the name of the person being bound all over it, while thinking—uh-uh, no more, buddy. This is the last crap anybody's going to take from your sorry self (or words to that effect). Take up some baling or binding twine or any available smallish string and wrap the entire egg with it, leaving none of the shell showing through. Tie the string off with strong little knots, and put the whole thing in the freezer for a moon cycle. At the end of that time, take the egg out and throw it into running water, like a river or big creek.

Marshmallow Hex

It's the sweetest little curse ever.

Here's what you need to gather up—the biggest marshmallows you can find, a felt-tipped pen, some long thorns or toothpicks. Write the name of the subject on the marshmallow as many times as will fit. Cover the entire surface. Then stick it with those thorns or toothpicks all over. Leave it outside for the ants and other insects to pick it apart, bit by bit. Just as you are "belittling" the person who has caused you harm.

Revenge: The War Bottle, with Staub

Because sometimes you've turned all the cheeks you possibly can turn.

This is a combo—a little mountain magic (staub) with a big borry out of the Afro-Caribbean traditions. Here's what you need to gather up: a jar (about quart-size—mayonnaise-jar sized) with a lid and a neck, your urine, your spit, long nails, your own dirt, dried hot peppers, big thorns, red dust, a few drops of your own blood.

This requires your commitment to seeing a hex through. Think about this a long, long time. Never mount or throw a war bottle in anger or fear. Never. No matter how pissed off you are or how important it is. Got that? You put all the above ingredients in a jar, fill the rest of the way with ditchwater (or other dirty water) and screw the top on tight. Drive a stout staub into the ground facing the direction of the person or persons for whom the jar is intended. Tie binding twine around the neck of the jar and tie the jar to the top of the staub (this may necessitate cutting a nick in the staub to tack up the twine). Now give it a gentle push to set the action in motion. Watch it swing back and forth for a few minutes while thinking of the person for whom the jar is intended. Don't be hateful—be easy. Just think of them going about their day, picture their face, think about the sound of her or his voice. Leave it there for a moon cycle—and I would start this working on Dark Moon—and let it do its work. When you're out in the yard, go by and give it a little push.

Word to the wise—this can be the end of a conflict, but it can also act as a declaration of war, if the object of the working is at all aware. Be prepared for enmity to ratchet up, so keep your personal shields intact, set strong wards around your property, and consider what the next move will be—either theirs or yours. Most people won't have the ability to do more than fume and freak out, but if you happen on someone who knows what they're doing, you'll need to be ready to lob some stuff back.

Or you might consider meeting with them, burying the hatchet, and learning how they do what they do. Friendly is always better, especially when everyone concerned has good boundaries.

FIRE ON THE MOUNTAIN

Weather patterns change. Now we blame global warming and overdevelopment, and in my youth, adults always wondered if the preacher had been properly paid. But whatever the reason, seasons aren't what they were when I was a child in west Buncombe County. It may be hard for newcomers to believe, but back in the 1960s, Enka-Candler was far away from the city of Asheville, so far away that children and grannies would venture out on Saturday morning to catch the Starnes Cove bus into town. The grannies warned us of strangers and cars, as though we'd never seen either. And when I was older—in high school—I'd come into town to visit my grandfather at his barbershop in the Flat Iron Building.

We were far from most city services out in the cove, but we did have city water whose pressure was so low by the time it got to the top of the hill that my dad built a concrete reservoir to catch enough of the drops to do laundry or wash dishes or take sponge baths in the kitchen. And in wet weather, there was a little stream that ran past the garden and the barn. My brother and I used to dam it up, and when the stream was running, we didn't have to carry buckets of water up the hill to the ponies. There was more rain when I was young, and the stream often saved our labor. I've been thinking about this a lot lately, as I haul buckets of gathered rainwater out to the eggplants and green beans, waiting for rains that are sporadic at best.

In the autumn of the year, we had dry days—a change from the afternoon thunderstorms of summer. We'd watch the process of the changing trees as we came up the road from school. The maples high on the mountain colored up first, and the rest followed in the fiery shades that brought the flatlanders up from wherever they lived to see "the color." I guess there were years of incredible glory when I was growing up, but that is not what I remember this time of year. When the trees start to change along Kimberley Avenue as I drive home from work, it's not the vivid orange or gold that brings it back to me. It's a smell, rare now in a world of lawn bags and vacuum-bearing trucks—the scent of dry burning leaves.

Our house was surrounded by woods and brush on three sides—a log and clapboard structure that lay uneasily at the top of a steep bank. To one side and above us were woods that connected directly to the shaggy back of the mountain. The kitchen door opened directly onto those woods, affording us cool breezes in the summer and visitations of possums, mice, and spiders—hairy and large—who carried their young upon their backs.

In the fall, we watched the skies at dusk to see if any wisps of smoke rose near us, gazing as far as Bensontown and Spivey to the left and Starnes Cove to the right. A wildfire on the mountain was a serious matter in those days when the only people who would likely be there to fight it were our daddies and our neighbors—men who had worked a full day and would work again tomorrow. Men whose experience in firefighting had more to do with burning off a field than suiting up in protective gear. I imagine there was a volunteer fire department somewhere, but I only remember the phone calls in the night as the men assembled with rakes and hoes and axes, going to take care of the fire. I would lie in my bed, watching the red glow through the window, smelling the smoke. I still sleep uneasily in the autumn, and I trace it to those fitful nights in the wooden house, listening for the phone, watching, sniffing the air.

There was always a chance that they couldn't stop the blaze, these subsistence farmers and truck drivers, especially in the driest of Octobers. We knew that we might have to take what belongings we could haul down the narrow steps beside the woods—the one-eyed bear, the sixty-four box of crayons—and load ourselves into the pink station wagon and get out of the cove.

We lived with nature then, and we knew that sometimes there was nothing to be done in the face of this immense and mostly uncontrollable force. Fire and wind, rain and ice. Often, with hard work and stubbornness, they were manageable and the crop was saved and the house still stood and the sick child did not die. But there were occasions when we bowed our heads to the inevitable and knew there were forces at work that were larger and more powerful than a hoe and a homemade tonic and a rake.

Now I live in a different world—developers can shear away great swaths of timber and stone and dirt and perch a multimillion-dollar home at the very top of a ridge, a home that can only be accessed by a SUV, shimmying its way up the switchbacks and curves of a paved drive. What happens to them during fire season, I wonder? Are they secure in the knowledge that they live in a safe and gated outpost, where rescue is only a 911 call away? I'd be willing to bet that they don't watch the ridgeline at dark or pace their wooden decks peering toward Bensontown. But I fancy that there might be a little girl, with her stuffed bear and a box of new crayons in a cardboard box under her bed, who lies in the darkness and smells an old scent—bitter and sweet—that grows stronger as the winds pick up.

But are they safer than we were? Maybe. Maybe trained firefighters can get up there and get them out in time. Maybe they have perimeter smoke detectors to warn them of impending wildfire. The nightly news brings us shocking footage from the drier heights of California—crying women clutching half-dressed babies, babbling about the wildfire that ate through their exclusive development.

As the drought lingers on here in the Appalachian Mountains, I again watch the sky at dusk, though Bensontown is too far away to matter now. I wonder about the homes on Spivey, the trailers that creep along the creek in Starnes Cove. Nature, as we often say but rarely heed, always bats last.

CHAPTER SIX

ON THE PORCH: SOME FRIENDLY ADVICE, A COUPLE OF STORIES, AND A GLASS OF SWEET TEA

Porches and front yards are important gathering places in these mountains. Passersby will be asked to come and sit and will be urged to stay. And stay. And stay. There is an old-fashioned sense of the obligations of hospitality, as well as the curiosity to hear the latest news and share a mutually remembered story, the telling of which often ends with "ay, law." Work was often done on the porch—outside where there was better light, in the fresh air. Looms and spinning wheels came out on fine days. Churning was done there too.

After our ramble through the landscape of hillfolks' hoodoo, we'll sit awhile on the porch and see where we've been and where we're likely to go next. Our porch is a place of rest, refreshment, and information sharing. As it should be. Have a seat.

As I write this final chapter, we are having a beautiful and too-early spring. The garden has kept me in its thrall for days, and I am rewarded with fresh salad greens and onions and more radishes than one person can possibly eat.

Spring is a time for renewal, for shaking off the winter doldrums, and the people in the southern Appalachians have a variety of things we do and eat to return to our lives outside in the fields and orchards. In spite of myself, I referenced Granny from the TV show *The Beverly Hillbillies*, and I'll reference her one last time. Doctor Granny was always trotting out some nasty spring tonic and dosing everybody in the family with it. Well, it turns out she was right. There are all kinds of delicious fresh greens that perk us up in the spring and early summer. I would be remiss in introducing my culture without encouraging you to try a few of those bright green allies, as you come to know this old culture and its traditions.

Do you remember the story of Rapunzel and why she was turned over at birth to the fabulous Witch-Architect who lived next door to her parents? It was because the pregnant mom-to-be was craving the beautiful rampion from the walled garden of said Witch-Architect, and Rapunzel's dad did a deal to get what the mom wanted. Ramps (*Allium tricoccum*) and rampion (*Campanula rapunculus*) are not the same, but when I was a child, I imagined the wide gold-green leaf and the fat white comma of the bulb on this familiar spring food. It lent a pungently visceral quality to the old story.

Last week, we began the spring nettle harvest, and they are a wonderful spring tonic. You can make soup of them, but I usually just steep a bunch of nettles into a strong tea, and I add a little honey to it and drink it over the course of a few days. I keep a big Mason jar of it in the fridge so it doesn't get funky, then heat it gently in a saucepan. Or sometimes I swig it out of the jar, cold from the fridge.

You do eat dandelions, don't you? I have always maintained that if people would simply eat all those weeds that are hard to remove from the perfect Stepford lawn, they'd be better off. When dandelions first break through the fog of my winter consciousness, I see them almost immediately and I begin to dream of harvesting them. Picking a mess of dandelion greens can be a big job because they cook down to nothing. But I pick them early and young and sauté them in a little olive oil and garlic.

Chickweed is another burst of green that happens in the early spring—so rich and lustrous that it is irresistible. Don't resist it. Pick it and munch on it, like a traveling salad. You can also use it in salad or soup, but I like it plain, as a walking/hiking snack.

I also eat a fair amount of violets—yes, the flowers—when they are in bloom. They are also good in salad or eaten plain.

And kudzu will be up and about soon. When I was growing up, we called it "kudgey vines." Use the tender young leaves just the way you would grape leaves. Stuff them with rice, and bake them in a nice broth. Or parboil them, wrap them around some good cheese, and put them under the broiler for a few minutes.

See? Some of my receipts really are recipes for healthful living, mountain-style. As you are learning to engage with the energy of the planet for your workings and to know the microclimate that is all around you (and upon which you also depend as a sign- and omen-reader), I hope you will realize the bright gift of fresh green things, whether as materials for talismans or as a way to recharge your personal battery.

These living traditions are always changing and evolving, and you are now part of that process. As you experiment and create, you will find that some things that work for me don't work for you. You may find a better way to do something that I've suggested. Good for you. And thanks for taking it all seriously enough to actually practice it. Many of you are reading this book for fun and insight into a place in which you're interested, but some of you will take all this to heart. I am grateful to you for that.

Let me warn you, though, to expect the unexpected. Your best intentions may sometimes be thwarted by the weather or a client or your own foggy head. Ground yourself, take a cool drink of water, and regroup. Try new things and different things and try them just for fun.

Scrying, like any esoteric technique, requires a lot of practice to be good at it. It's a matter of unfocusing your eyes (at least it is for me and for most people I know who practice it) as you clear your mind.

In an earlier chapter, we discussed this as a divination method, but it is also used for "overlooking"—viewing something that is happening far away from your physical surroundings. I'll give you an example.

My divination method of choice, as you know, is tarot. I've been reading cards for about forty years and am very comfortable with that technique. Several years ago, however, I decided that a witch ought to be able to read a crystal ball too. It seemed like a bit of boffo I'd be wise to adopt.

I hadn't read a ball since I was a child and was sent home from Sunday School for dressing as a "Gypsy" for Hallowe'en and bringing my crystal ball—my grandmother's water globe—to class. I was told it was an "inappropriate costume." Little did those sweet Methodist ladies know how totally inappropriate I would later become.

I had taught myself scrying and used those techniques on a heavy globe that was a gift from a friend. I read for a few folks and then brought it to a psychic fair fund-raiser for a local nonprofit. I was reading the ball for someone I didn't know, and what I saw was a little movie playing out in the smooth curve of the crystal. I described it to the woman sitting across from me.

"There's a fireplace and a chair in front of it and another chair beside it."

"That's my living room."

"There's a kind of old frayed rug in front of the fireplace and a cat in the chair."

"What does the cat look like?"

"Brown and white."

"That's Buster—is he in the chair?"

"Yes."

"That stinker! I'll kill him when I get home. He knows he's not supposed to be there."

It kept going on like that for a while. She was disappointed that I couldn't tell her the future, but she thought it was cool that I could see her house.

So don't be surprised if you see pictures the very first time—try not to let it freak you out. Keep practicing and playing with it. I confess I don't practice nearly enough, but I do enjoy it. Though I sometimes wish I had my grandmother's old globe. Wonder whatever happened to that?

I hope you've learned a bit about where I come from and the kind of rootwork we do here. Hillfolks' hoodoo isn't especially fancy, it doesn't require expensive materials, but it does require you to practice it, darn near all the time. As you know from these pages, you don't need to ever work with clients if you choose not to—it is perfectly appropriate to use all these techniques for grounding, energy working, and divination to aid you in your studies and work.

Feel free to find yourself a parking space downtown, to set up a little open purse abundance spell when you're needing extra resources, to make and wear a sachet in your pocket when you need some extra luck.

This is a primer, a beginner's guide to all this material. It gives you some things to start practicing and doing, but it isn't the last word on this folk-magic system. But if you practice the techniques in this book and use your imagination, you will have plenty to do.

As we leave the companionship of the porch, you may wonder—where do we go from here? The usual answer is—home. The passerby or the visitor will stretch and say—better get to the house. I will reply with—best stay for supper. We will begin the back and forth of chores to be done and folks to see, even as you step off the porch and head home.

These are homely arts, after all. Most can be done at the kitchen table or at your workbench on the porch. The requirements are few, and you have this little primer to guide you, if need be.

As you start down your own path, rambling toward home, you'll remember that attitude is everything, that practice makes perfect and that it is always good to mind your manners. Unless provoked. You may recall that some plants may be picked as you walk home, harvested for later use. You'll look forward to home, and a cool drink of sweet water.

You may choose to further your education through more books, a workshop, or the like. There are workshops available in person—the whole Hillfolks' Hoodoo series repeats a couple of times a year. If you are in western North Carolina or visiting, please check my website for information or send me an email note. There are also some distance-learning opportunities online.

We've included a few blank pages for your own receipts and experiments in the old and new practice of this strain of Appalachian folk magic. I hope you will continue to be curious, to practice for yourself and for others, to believe that attitude is important in this as in life. And if you gained a little respect for this old and fading culture in the process, then another little job of work is done.

Get on home now. Let me know if you need me.

GLOSSARY

Boffo: A touch of flair and drama that engages the client in the work (from Terry Pratchett).

Borry: Something borrowed from a different tradition. Florida water is a borry.

Canning: A method of preserving food for future consumption, canning involves preparing, settling into jars, and heating to seal the jars.

Canning lids, rings, jars: The tools of canning, these are used to store, prepare and transport herbs and tinctures.

Cauldron: A heavy round cooking pot, often cast iron, sometimes used for laundry.

Cove doctor: Another word for someone who practices mountain healing and folk magic. Sometimes called a yarb (herb) woman, often not called anything at all.

Divination: The art of purposefully looking into the future.

Do-rag or head-rag: Cloth head covering. You put this on when you have some work to do.

Dolly: A poppet, a small human image made of cloth, wood or other materials.

Earth-based: A spiritual system that has at its core a

veneration for the earth. The solstices and equinoxes, as well as the midpoint between them, are observed.

Folkways: Traditional customs of a particular social group.

Funeral Home Fan: Used to be common in small churches, these are advertisements in the form of heavy paper hand fans.

Hoodoo: The practice of folk magic.

Intuition: What you know in the pit of your stomach; that small voice of your inner wisdom.

Ken: A Scots phrase that means to have knowledge of or understanding about something.

Moon cycle: From one phase of the moon until that same phase comes again, in about a month. It's a convenient way to keep track of time.

New fire: Fire struck from flint and steel or with a magnifying glass; fire that doesn't come from other fire.

Omen: Something natural, observed and unusual.

Poppet: See Dolly.

Premonition: A sign or omen that usually indicates something dire.

Primer: A small book that covers the basics of a particular subject.

Ramble: A curious and easy walk through the woods or the fields or the whole wide world.

Receipt: A formula or recipe for a working or material.

Redding: Brick dust or the dust from red clay mud that has been dried and pulverized.

Rootwork: Cross-cultural folk magic.

Rootworker: Someone who practices rootwork.

Sachet: A small packet that contains herbs and charms for healing.

Scry: A divination technique that features peering into a reflective surface, like a crystal ball or a still pool.

Seven-day/glass jar candles: A candle contained in a tall glass jar. Sometimes they have images and prayers on them.

Sign: Something natural and observed.

Spring water: Fresh water that comes from a spring; bottled spring water can also be used.

SUGGESTED BIBLIOGRAPHY AND RESOURCES

Andrews, Ted. *Nature-Speak: Signs, Omens and Messages in Nature*

Baron-Reid, Colette. *Messages from Spirit: The Extraordinary Power of Oracles, Omens, and Signs*

Bascom, William Russell. *Ifa Divination: Communication between Gods and Men in West Africa*

Bluestone, Sarvananda. *How to Read Signs and Omens in Everyday Life*

Cunningham, Scott. *Divination for Beginners*

Fiery, Ann. *The Book of Divination*

John, Michael. *The Art and Practice of Geomancy*

Hunt, Victoria. *Animal Omens*

Krasskova, Galina. *Runes: Theory and Practice*

Matthews, Caitlin. *Celtic Wisdom Sticks*

Nelson, John. *The Magic Mirror: Divination through the Ancient Art of Scrying*

Paxson, Diana. *Taking Up the Runes*

Peirce, Penney. *The Intuitive Way: The Definitive Guide to Increasing Your Awareness*

Rago, Linda. *Blackberry Cove Herbal: Healing with Common Herbs*

Reed, Henry. *Awakening Your Psychic Powers: Open Your Inner Mind and Control Your Psychic Intuition Today*

Richmond, Nancy. *Appalachian Folklore Omens, Signs and Superstitions*

Rosanoff, Nancy. *Intuition Workout: A Practical Guide to Discovering and Developing Your Inner Knowing*

Hex Magazine Hoodoo and Conjure Quarterly

Resources:

Dorothy Morrison www.dorothymorrison.com

Judika Illes www.judikailles.com

Orion Foxwood www.orionfoxwood.com

And my site—www.myvillagewitch.com

ABOUT THE AUTHOR

H. Byron Ballard is a native of western North Carolina and lives in Asheville. She has a MFA from Trinity University in theatre and a BA from UNC-Asheville in drama. She is a ritualist, teacher, speaker and writer. Byron has been a practicing Witch since the early 1970s and a Wiccan priestess since 1975.

Her published writing has appeared in *WNC Woman, Mountain Xpress, Carolina Home & Garden, Verve Magazine, Witches and Pagans, PanGaia* and the *Black Mountain Review*. Her essays are featured in *Birthed from Scorched Hearts* ("The Daughters of Boudicca"), Fulcrum Press; *Christmas Presence* ("A Season of Light: How We Celebrated a Hillbilly Yule") Catawba Press; *Clothes Lines* edited by Miles and Dillingham, Catawba Press; *Women's Spaces, Women's Places* edited by Miles and Dillingham, Stone Ivy Press; *Which Witch is Which* by Patricia Telesco, New Page Books; *Into the Great Below*, edited by Galina Krasskova, Asphodel Press.

She has essays and articles on Wicca and other earth-focused spiritualities at *The Witches Voice* website, *Global Goddess Oracle* e-zine, and *Matrifocus*.

She blogged as "The Village Witch" for the local Gannett daily and can be reached via email at info@ myvillagewitch.com. Find her on Facebook and Twitter as well.

Website: www.myvillagewitch.com

RECEIPTS AND NOTES

RECEIPTS AND NOTES

CPSIA information can be obtained
at www.ICGtesting.com
Printed in the USA
JSHW080148100523
41502JS00004B/30